Praise for

Gift-Wrapped by God

"In *Gift-Wrapped by God* Linda Dillow and Lorraine Pintus creatively weave together Scripture and the personal experiences of single women to offer a radical alternative to contemporary notions of sexual fulfillment."

—PEGGY WEHMEYER, journalist

"*Gift-Wrapped by God* offers pearls of wisdom for those beginning the journey to womanhood as well as those struggling between the balance of purity and dealing with their desires. It also provides rivers of restoration for those who live with regret over past mistakes."

—MICHELLE MCKINNEY HAMMOND, author of *Get Over It and On With It*

"Gifted encouragers, Linda and Lorraine not only build a powerful case for the reasons God asks singles to wait for sex, they also provide lots of specific, practical advice for how. The accompanying Bible study will enable readers to integrate and apply the liberating message of this book."

—DENNIS RAINEY, executive director of FamilyLife

"Whatever has been your sexual experience and wherever you are on your spiritual journey, this powerful book will give you God's perspective and set you free from guilt and shame."

—NEY BAILEY, speaker and author of *Faith Is Not a Feeling*

"This real love story strikes a chord that will resound in the hearts of all women. It is more than an admonition to live pure lives. It reveals the beauty of being created feminine and the precious gift that has been entrusted to all women, single and married."

—PASTOR TED and GAYLE HAGGARD, New Life Church, Colorado Springs

"Linda and Lorraine give us hope as they describe and illustrate the wonderful and perfect plan of God in saving the gift of sexuality."

—PHYLLIS and PAUL STANLEY, international vice president of The Navigators

"*Gift-Wrapped by God* does an excellent job of reminding us that there is always a fresh start for those who feel that they have given away the 'gift' prematurely. That the mercies of Jesus Christ are new every morning—this may be the ultimate gift!"

—KELLY MINTER, songwriter and recording artist

"Linda Dillow and Lorraine Pintus write with conviction, warmth, and great pragmatism in *Gift-Wrapped by God*. Rarely does an author balance great admonition to live a godly life with great forgiveness for those who have gone astray, but these authors accomplish that."

—FRANK MINIRTH, PH.D., author of *Happiness Is a Choice* and
Worry-Free Living

"Millions of young women and men have been defrauded of their sexual purity by a culture that has exalted rights over responsibility, pleasure over purity, sensuality over self-control, and today over tomorrow. *Gift-Wrapped by God* is a gift to this defrauded generation. It speaks healing, forgiveness, wholeness, encouragement, and wisdom. Linda and Lorraine impart a biblical outlook on sexuality that will change the way you think about yourself, your sexuality, your past, your future, and your partner—and most important your God."

—DR. DAVID E. SCHROEDER, president of Nyack College/
Alliance Theological Seminary

"*Gift-Wrapped by God* is a must-read book for single women everywhere. This straightforward book gets to the heart of the issue of sexual purity."

—PASTOR MIKE MACINTOSH, Horizon Christian Fellowship,
San Diego, California

Gift-Wrapped by God

Secret Answers to the Question "Why Wait?"

LINDA DILLOW & LORRAINE PINTUS

WATERBROOK
PRESS

GIFT-WRAPPED BY GOD
PUBLISHED BY WATERBROOK PRESS
12265 Oracle Boulevard, Suite 200
Colorado Springs, Colorado 80921
A division of Random House, Inc.

All Scripture quotations, unless otherwise noted, are taken from the *New American Standard Bible*® (NASB). © Copyright The Lockman Foundation 1960, 1962, 1963, 1968, 1971, 1972, 1973, 1975, 1977, 1995. Used by permission. (www.Lockman.org). Scripture quotations marked (MSG) are taken from *The Message*. Copyright © by Eugene H. Peterson 1993, 1994, 1995. Used by permission of NavPress Publishing Group. Scripture quotations marked (NIV) are taken from the *Holy Bible, New International Version*®. NIV®. Copyright © 1973, 1978, 1984 by International Bible Society. Used by permission of Zondervan Publishing House. All rights reserved. Scripture quotations marked (NKJV) are taken from the *New King James Version*. Copyright © 1982 by Thomas Nelson, Inc. Used by permission. All rights reserved. Scripture quotations marked (NLT) are taken from *The Holy Bible, New Living Translation,* copyright © 1996. Used by permission of Tyndale House Publishers, Inc., Wheaton, Illinois 60189. All rights reserved. Scripture quotations marked (NRSV) are taken from *The New Revised Standard Version of the Bible,* copyright © 1989 by the Division of Christian Education of the National Council of the Churches of Christ in the USA. Used by permission. All rights reserved. Scripture quotations marked (KJV) are taken from the *King James Version*.

Details in some anecdotes and stories have been changed to protect the identities of the persons involved.

ISBN 1-4000-7077-5

The Library of Congress has cataloged the hardcover edition as follows:
Dillow, Linda.
  Gift-wrapped by God : secret answers to the question "why wait?" / Linda Dillow and Lorraine
Pintus. — 1st ed.
    p. cm.
  ISBN 1-57856-585-5
  1. Chastity. 2. Youth—Religious life. 3. Marriage—Religious aspects—Christianity. 4. Sexual abstinence—Religious aspects—Christianity. I. Pintus, Lorraine. II. Title.
  BV4647.C5 D55 2002
  241'.66—dc21

                                                            2002006904

Printed in the United States of America
2006

10 9 8 7 6 5 4 3 2

To my precious granddaughters,
Annika and Sofia,
and the ones yet to come
LINDA

To my darling daughters,
Amanda and Megan
LORRAINE

We wrote this for you because it is the book
we wish we'd had as young women.

Contents

Acknowledgments

This book sings because of the many voices who have joined its chorus.

First, a heartfelt thank-you to Liz Heaney, our super editor whose prayers and giftedness helped form this book. We love you, Liz! We are grateful to you and to the wonderful staff at WaterBrook for their vision and commitment to the message of sexual purity.

We'd also like to thank the women who graciously gave us permission to tell their stories—Kendall, Natalie, Darcy, Nancy, Patti Ann, Jill, Patti, and many others who openly and honestly shared their hurts and joys with us.

Thanks to the young women across America who field-tested the book and Bible study: Mauri Brindle and her New Life interns, Becca Wesselink and her Campus Crusaders, Beth Lubbe and her Navigators, Linda Kitchen at Great Commission Ministry and her high school group, and Bethany Harling and her friends at Houghton College. Your collective wisdom provided rich insight and practical help.

Our deep appreciation also goes to Don and Cathy Couchman and Don and Peggy Hanley, who provided writing retreats for us.

We praise God for each of you and especially for our long-suffering husbands, Jody and Peter, who once again supported and encouraged us throughout this intensive time of prayer and writing.

Finally, and most important, we want to express supreme gratitude to Jesus Christ, our Lord and Savior and the lover of our souls. May all who dwell in these pages fall more deeply in love with You, our eternal bridegroom.

Dear friend,

This book is about God's plan for sexual purity and His heart for you, His daughter. It's the book we wish we'd had when we were single, because we believe it would have saved us much heartache.

As you read, may your eyes be lifted to the beauty of God's Gift of sex. May you discover emotional and spiritual reasons why sex is worth the wait. If you have already given away the Gift, may you receive hope of a new beginning sexually.

Thousands of women have shared with us their deep regret concerning their wrong sexual choices. Repeatedly we hear, "I wish someone had told me to say no, told me why to say no, and helped me develop my own plan to say no." We pray that Gift-Wrapped by God will do this for you.

Know that we are praying for you. May God speak to your heart with each page you turn.

Linda &
Lorraine

www.intimateissues.com

~

The Gift

Chapter 1

Confusing Voices

Mandy grabbed a bagel, picked up her stack of books, and headed out the front door. As she paused to pick up the morning newspaper, a headline blared:

CONGRESSMAN HAS SEX WITH INTERN

When she got on the freeway, traffic was at a standstill. Why hadn't she taken the back roads? She drummed her fingers on the steering wheel impatiently and read the bumper sticker on the car in front of her:

WANTED: MEANINGFUL OVERNIGHT RELATIONSHIP
WITH MEMBER OF OPPOSITE SEX.

When Mandy finally slid into the back row of her philosophy class, she was only two minutes late. Her professor had scribbled the homework assignment on the white board. She was supposed to write a two-page report on:

THE POSITIVE IMPACT OF THE GAY COMMUNITY
ON ARTS AND HUMANITIES

Later, as she nursed a latte at Starbucks, Mandy looked out the window. She couldn't miss the two large billboards on the side of the building across the street. One showed a man and woman intertwined in a passionate kiss over a bottle of scotch while the one next to it shouted:

JUST DO IT.

A few hours later Mandy mopped sweat from her brow after a grueling workout at The Body Shop. Blaire, a brassy brunette she'd known for a few months, sidled up to her in a skimpy workout suit that created five cases of whiplash from the guys around her. After a short greeting, Blaire asked Mandy if she was going to the big party Saturday night. Mandy knew the theme of the party: Decadence 'til Dawn. "Don't think so," she said. In a voice loud enough for others to hear, Blaire quipped:

"You must be the only virgin left on this planet."

That evening, after finishing her report, Mandy curled up on the sofa and clicked on the television. A sitcom rerun fired sexual innuendos with the rapidity of a machine gun, and couples casually hopped in and out of bed. Grabbing the remote, Mandy punched Off and opted instead for a mind-numbing woman's magazine. The cover's main headline screamed:

SIX WAYS TO SEDUCE YOUR BOYFRIEND

As Mandy crawled into bed that night, a scoreboard in her mind flashed:

World's Messages on Sex: 35
God's Messages on Sex: 0

SEXUAL SATURATION

We live in a sex-crazed society. A lengthy article in *USA Today* describes how twenty-five thousand single professionals flock to an East Coast beach town each Friday for their "weekly rite of regression." Their goal: To escape the shackles of responsibility through "I don't care" encounters that involve sex and alcohol.[1] Another *USA Today* article talks about the current trend for couples to "hook up." According to the article, "Hookups are defined by alcohol, physical attraction and a lack of expectations in the morning."[2]

At no other time in history have women been so bombarded with sexual misinformation and anti-God messages about their sexuality. Our culture has adopted a Sodom-and-Gomorrah mentality that is promoted on everything from cereal boxes to satellites. In a thousand different ways through a thousand different venues, over and over and over the message blares: "Do it anywhere, anytime, with anyone." But wait! Another voice cries (with a hint of piousness), "Do it anywhere, anytime, with anyone, but make sure you have a condom in your pocket."

Frustrated, Christian women look to the church in hopes of finding clear answers that will silence the noisy chaos clamoring in their ears. Here the voices are different, but sometimes they are just as confusing:

Don't date.

Do date.

Don't kiss.

Kiss, but don't use your tongues.

Don't have sex until you are married. (the spoken message)

Don't have sex until you really, really love someone
and can't handle the sexual tension any longer.
(the frequently modeled message)

The new leader of your singles group (the last one was dismissed due to a "sexual indiscretion") points to several scriptures and talks about the importance of waiting. Heads bob up and down in agreement, including the head of the girl you know is sleeping with her boyfriend. Part of you accedes, "Waiting is right." Another part of you argues, "Sexual purity is possible if you are a missionary in the jungle, but what if you are a paralegal in a law office full of attractive men?"

Conflicting, confusing voices shout at you from every direction. It's enough to drive a woman crazy! Who should you listen to? How do you know which voices to follow and which ones to tune out?

Amidst the cacophony of voices, we invite you to calm your heart, still your thoughts, and open your ears. Another voice speaks. A quiet voice. A wise voice. The voice of Truth. The voice of God.

Your heavenly Father, the One who loves you and created you as a sexual being, wants you to hear His voice. Right now He is calling you. Will you come?

Open your ears. Open your heart. God wants to speak to you.

Come, My daughter.
Come with Me.
I want to take you back to the beginning
   Back before the confusing voices,
   Back to creation.
Gaze upon the man and the woman.
Each is My masterpiece, each an exquisite
     work of art.
It is My plan to unite the two and make them
     one.
How will I do this?
I will give the man and the woman a Gift,
    a Gift they can give to one another.
   The Gift is beautiful.
     The Gift is wrapped in pleasure.
      The Gift is holy.
       Very, very holy.

Chapter 2

God's Masterpiece

The angelic host that encircled the Creator watched with hushed fascination as He caressed Adam's rib in His hands. The Almighty lovingly trailed His finger along the smooth surface, then smiled as He set about sculpting the beautiful creature He had already fashioned in His mind.

The angels sang softly as He shaped, stretched, and then connected bone upon bone to weave a lovely form. Before the day's final shadows had fallen, He had designed an intricate network of all things vital to life and covered it with a smooth fabric of skin.

ANGEL   She is smaller and more delicate than the man.

GOD   Yes, but I have knit into her being undeniable strength.

ANGEL   And she is much softer. Her body, her hair…

GOD   Ahhh—the softness is part of the fascination.

ANGEL   Her body dents in and out!

GOD   I call these curves. They are part of the softness.

ANGEL   Her body flows—so unlike the man's.

GOD   The two are designed differently so they might fit together as one.

ANGEL   Can she feel?

GOD   Oh yes! She feels deeply; joy, love, sorrow. And exquisite pleasure.

ANGEL   Pleasure?

GOD   Pleasure awaits her, hidden deep within, beneath the soft folds. Yet all of her delicate skin responds to touch.

ANGEL	Lord, You out did Yourself with this creation. She is a work of art.
GOD	Yes, but she is also a gift. I have wrapped her and sealed her within her body to protect her until the Day of Celebration when the man will unwrap her.
ANGEL	The Day of Celebration?
GOD	It is called The Wedding.
ANGEL	How long must she wait until the unwrapping?
GOD	Sometimes it is a very long time.
ANGEL	It must be difficult to wait.
GOD	Yes…very hard. But the unveiling is worth the wait. When the wrappings come off and the woman's seal is broken, the man and the woman will delight in a love overflowing with…

> intimate oneness,
>> unique knowledge,
>>> exquisite pleasure,
>>>> holy wonder.
>>>>> This love is my Gift to them.

Chapter 3

Tira: One Woman's Reflections

Many young brides have shared their stories with us. Tira's story is a fiction-alized composite of their experiences.

I stood before the ornately carved doors, swathed in a cloud of white satin and pearls, tightly gripping my father's arm. We exchanged nervous smiles and said in unison, "Ready."

The doors swung open. The first chords of the wedding march echoed off the lofty ceiling as two hundred people rose to their feet. Slowly, we made our way up the aisle.

The faces on both sides of us reflected my own joy. Stacy, my grade-school friend, stood next to dear Aunt Nelda, who beamed at me from beneath her flouncy pink hat. Wanda, my office manager, stood beside my high-school track coach, who gave me a thumbs-up signal. One row was filled with college friends; another overflowed with relatives from distant cities. Then, near the front, the smiles of my new family welcomed me. In that moment time stopped. It was as if my past and present had merged together to witness my future.

Then I lifted my eyes and connected with my husband-to-be's dark eyes, eyes that drank me in with one look. Every other face slipped into oblivion as I mounted the steps and slipped my hand into his.

~

I stood before Russ, draped in a simple, low-cut, white silk negligee held together by three satin ribbons that tied in the front. I smiled shyly as I watched him study the curves of my body beneath the clingy fabric.

"Tira, Tira, you take my breath away…," he sighed, and I could see the longing in his eyes.

"I'd prefer, handsome gentleman, that you address me as Mrs. Russell Westcott," I teased.

"As you wish, Mrs. Westcott," he replied with an exaggerated bow of respect. "Anything else my lady desires? Anything at all?"

His boyish grin was part teasing, part caress. How does he do that? How does he embrace me without physically touching me?

"I desire *you*," I whispered.

"And I, Mrs. Westcott…desire *you*." Pulling me into his arms, he kissed me, tenderly at first, and then with a mounting passion that infused liquid warmth through my body. A sweet ache filled me as I melted into him, marveling at how our bodies seemed to mold together. It was as if we were two separate pieces of one whole.

My heart beat wildly with expectation. It seemed as if I had spent a lifetime waiting, planning for this moment. I pushed myself from Russ's embrace and took one step away from him.

"I have a Gift for you, Mr. Westcott." Curious, he arched his brow quizzically and waited for me to continue.

Opening my arms slightly, I smiled and said, "I'm your gift. Why don't you come and unwrap me?"

Tears filled his eyes as he reached forward and slowly, very slowly, pulled at the end of the satin until the twist of the bow slipped away.

~

I stood on the sandy beach and watched as my husband of three days jogged near the pounding surf. *MY HUSBAND.* Russ was no longer simply a best friend; he had become intimately mine. I knew Russ in ways no one had ever known him. I smiled as thoughts of how we had awakened each other this morning filled me with silent wonderment.

Sex was wonderful, but it was only one aspect of the joy I was feeling. Before Russ and I were married, things like going to lunch together or shopping for a new shirt seemed mundane. Now even those things suddenly had a new intimacy. It's as if I could feel God's hand of blessing on everything we did. I sensed a settled-down peace in my spirit that whispered, "This is right. This is as it should be."

Thank You, God. I'm so happy. Thank You for protecting me
from all the wrong choices I could have made.
I'm so grateful that I have no regrets,
no other faces to intrude on my oneness with Russ.

As I strolled along the water's edge, breathing in the warm sun and salt water, I thought about my friend who had chosen to give herself all the privileges of marriage without a commitment. I wondered, *Does she wake up with the same feeling of awe...the same fluttery anticipation...the same irrepressible grin that this man beside her is her very own forever? I don't think so.*

My reflections ended as Russ bounded toward me like a wet puppy wanting to play.

"My lady looks hot. I think a splash in the ocean would cool you off."

"Russ, no! This is my new sarong. I don't want it full of salt water."

"That's Mr. Westcott, SIR, to you, Mrs. Westcott." He grabbed me and threw me over his shoulder as I screamed in mock protest. As he hauled me toward the crashing waves, my spirit welled up within me. *Thank You, Lord. Thank You.*

Chapter 4

The Gift Exchange

Both of us love Christmas because it's a time to give and receive gifts. When we were little, we waited in agony for the day to arrive when we could finally open the packages under the tree. We'd shake the boxes, trying to figure out what was in them. When no one was looking, we peeled away candy-cane paper to see what was inside and then carefully taped over the lifted corners so no one would discover our crime. Weeks before Christmas, we climbed under beds and investigated closet corners to find out if our parents had been paying attention when we'd recited our wish list.

When we finally open a gift, the curiosity, the anticipation, and the waiting help to make the gift more meaningful. The way a gift is wrapped can also make it meaningful, especially when it is wrapped in sacrifice.

Lorraine: Money was scarce the first Christmas Peter and I were married. We agreed we would not spend more than ten dollars on our gifts for each other. Imagine my shock when I opened his gift to me—a deluxe blender with six special attachments!

"You *promised* you wouldn't spend more than ten dollars," I accused.

"I didn't," he said. "I used the money I got from selling my sports racquet to make up the difference."

Giving this gift had cost my husband plenty since playing racquetball was one of his passions. Almost twenty-five years later, I still have my Christmas blender.

Linda: I remember the year I sold blood so that I could purchase a special set of books that Jody desperately wanted. Even after giving pints of blood, I was still short of the cost of the books. But the Lord was gracious, and the books went on sale the week before Jody's birthday. What joy to give him a gift literally purchased with my own blood!

Both of these gifts were wrapped in the tender paper of sacrifice. Don't you love a package that has been personally wrapped? The gift-wrap is an invitation, a promise of what lies beneath the wrapping.

You have seen that God created the Gift of sex for married couples, but did you know that *you are a Gift* and that God has personally wrapped you? Before you came from your dark comfort into the light of the world, God fashioned and skillfully knit you together. He wove together an authentic personality with choice characteristics unlike any other creation. He established plans and purposes just for you. Then He wrapped you in a design of His own unique choosing.

Some women are wrapped in a creative container that arouses curiosity and imagination in the heart of the one to whom they will give the Gift. Others are wrapped in simple paper, accentuated with a shimmering ribbon, a signature of their individuality. Sometimes the wrapping is sleek—a satiny cover that reflects God's resplendent light. Other times the wrapping is honest earthiness—a burlap case adorned with a bright crimson bow and whimsical, woodsy twigs.

God wraps each Gift individually. Each is uniquely beautiful. Each is sealed and marked with a tag in His own handwriting: Do not open until…

THE CELEBRATION

God knew the delight of a gift wrapped to entice the eye and give joy to the chosen one, so He took the Gift called *You* and intricately wove His most exquisite wrapping round and round your form.

In chapter 2 we saw how God gift-wrapped Eve at creation. Next we entered into the joy of Tira's wedding celebration as she gave the Gift of her body to her husband the night of their wedding. Now we'll reflect on the beauty of the Gift Exchange.

THE GIFT EXCHANGE

Hidden in a passage of Scripture is the picture of the Gift Exchange.

> The wife gives authority over her body to her husband, and
> the husband also gives authority over his body to his wife.
> (1 Corinthians 7:4, NLT)

On your wedding night, you and your new husband will exchange the most priceless gift, the Gift of your bodies. Until this time, your bodies belonged to each of you and to God. On this special night, you give your beloved authority over your body, and he gives you authority over his body. What an awesome privilege and responsibility to give and receive this Gift!

One new bride explained the Gift Exchange this way:

> I felt like I repeated my vows twice. In the afternoon, I gave my
> public vow before hundreds of people to love, honor, and cherish,
> but that evening when I came out of the bathroom in my silky,
> skimpy negligee, I gave a private vow that was just for the ears and
> eyes of my husband. I can't remember the exact words, but it went
> something like this: "I have a Gift for you—a Gift God wrapped
> and I valued highly enough to save for you. The Gift is my body. I
> give it to you tonight and my desire is to…"
>
> I had planned to say more but got interrupted when my hus-
> band grabbed me and threw his arms around me so tightly I could
> hardly breathe. No more words were needed…
>
> Was our first time perfect? No. As I look back, I realize we
> were actually a bit nervous and clumsy with each other, but we've
> been married four months now and the clumsiness and nervous-
> ness are gone. I've learned what it means to have a "unique knowl-
> edge" of every part of the Gift he gave me. There is such fun, such
> indescribable joy, and such freedom.

Our prayer is that you will know this same joy and freedom.

GOD'S BLESSING

Come with us into the pages of Scripture and see God's picture of the Gift Exchange with another bride who waited. Amazingly, we are invited to view a very private scene in the life of Solomon and his new bride. The wedding celebration is over, the guests have gone home, and the couple is alone in the bridal chamber in the palace.[1]

Electricity fills the air as the groom approaches his beloved. "Your lips, my bride, drip honey; honey and milk are under your tongue" (Song of Solomon 4:11). His eyes move longingly over her body. "You are altogether beautiful, my darling" (4:7).

Sexual tension mounts as the groom whispers, "You have made my heart beat faster…, my bride; you have made my heart beat faster with a single glance of your eyes" (4:9). Then, marveling that he would be the first person to explore her virgin body and its treasures, he says, "A garden[2] locked is…my bride,…a spring sealed up" (4:12). Passion fills the bride, and she invites, "May my beloved come into his garden and eat its choice fruits!" (4:16).

As the newlyweds lie entwined in sexual oneness, heat emanating from their bodies, the scene is suddenly suspended. A third Person enters the bed chamber. In a tender benediction that reveals His great delight over what has just taken place, the Creator walks over to the bridal bed and extends His hand of blessing over the couple with these words:

Eat, friends; drink and imbibe deeply, O lovers. (5:1)

The Sovereign Lord of the universe, the Majestic God of all creation, urges a husband and a wife to give the Gift of their bodies to one another and to drink deeply of His Gift to them—the Gift of sexual love.

An old Anglican wedding vow crystallizes the beauty of this Gift Exchange. Over a hundred years ago, a bride and groom publicly declared their intent to exchange the Gift of their bodies with these stirring words:

With my body, I thee worship.
My body will adore Thee.
And your body alone will I cherish
I will with my body declare your worth.[3]

Can you imagine yourself saying these words out loud before hundreds of people? Men and women would squirm in their seats, and you would blush from head to toe. Yet these words are holy—they express God's heart about sexual love.

What are your thoughts? Do you see the holiness, the beauty, and the passion that are part of the Gift Exchange? Have your eyes been lifted to the glory of God's perspective? Join us in praying:

> *God, thank You for the beauty of the Gift Exchange.*
> *Continue to deepen in me the idea that the Gift of sex is holy.*
> *Teach me Your perspective.*
> *Let me hear Your voice and Yours alone.*

Chapter 5

God's Voice on Sex

Perhaps you have heard God's voice in some areas of your life, but do you know His voice when it comes to matters of intimacy? In the last chapter you heard Him speak of His delight when a husband and wife give the Gift of their bodies to one another. But what else does God say about sexual intimacy?

Let us take you deeper into God's Word. We read the Bible from Genesis to Revelation and found hidden in Scripture six reasons why God gave the Gift of sexual passion to married couples. We also discovered a beautiful portrait of a young bride who lived out God's intentions. Delve with us into the pages of God's Word and let Him speak to you.

SIX REASONS WHY GOD GAVE THE GIFT OF SEX[1]

God Declares: "I Gave the Gift of Sex That You Might Create Life."[2]
We see so many pregnant women that we sometimes take having a baby for granted. But can you imagine Eve? She had never seen another pregnant woman. Can you picture the expression of bewilderment on her face when her stomach started to grow...and grow and grow! Turning to her heavenly Father, she exclaimed, "I think I'm going to explode!"

With a knowing smile He replied, "Just wait, Eve. The miracle of new life is in the making...inside of you!"

Imagine Eve's awestruck wonder when she gave birth to her first child. Mystery and heaven came together on earth as she held her baby boy in her arms.

The Gift of sex may also one day give you the privilege of joining with God in creating life. Your love plus your husband's love can create a child. Through sexual union—and only through this union—an eternal being is created. The angels in heaven must stand in awe that God would entrust us with so great a Gift.

God Declares: "I Gave the Gift of Sex for Intimate Oneness."

We asked young women what came to their minds when they heard the word *intimacy,* and they said:

"Bonded together."

"Linked closely."

"Oneness in body, soul, and spirit."

God made us to be creatures who crave intimate connection. We yearn for someone who knows us, who understands us completely, and who will love us to the core of our being. We desire intimacy with God but also with someone who will walk through life with us.

In Ephesians 5, the apostle Paul talks about a type of intimacy he calls a mystery.

> For this reason a man shall leave his father and mother and shall be joined to his wife, and the two shall become one flesh. This mystery is great; but I am speaking with reference to Christ and the church. (Ephesians 5:31-32)

What is the great mystery? That somehow a husband and wife coming together in sexual intercourse is a reference to Christ and the church. As we meditated on these verses, we became convinced that this would be an accurate paraphrase:

> On your wedding night when you and your bridegroom become one sexually, you will experience the most intimate physical act on this earth. When you taste of the knit-together closeness and experience the melting together of your bodies, you will then have

a visual picture of the spiritual closeness that the Lord Jesus wants with you.

This boggles the mind! Women say to us, "But Linda and Lorraine, isn't sex very fleshly? The sights, the sounds, the passion—it just isn't very spiritual. Are you sure this is what God meant?"

Yes, we're sure. God made us physical beings, and in Scripture He often uses physical pictures to explain spiritual truths. He placed a bleeding, screaming sacrificial lamb on an altar and said:

Look, this is a picture of the Lamb of God who will one day take away the sins of the world.

He takes two aching bodies entwined in ecstasy and says:

Look, this is a picture of the spiritual bonding I long to have with you.

Do you grasp what God is saying? From His perspective, sexual oneness in marriage is so beautiful, so holy, so intimate that He compares it to spiritual oneness.

Read through this section again before you go any further. Most people do not understand that sexual intimacy really is a great mystery, and it takes time to digest this glorious truth.

God Declares: "I Gave the Gift of Sex for a Unique Knowledge."
The Hebrew word for sexual intercourse is the word for "to know."[3] Through God's Gift of sex, you and your husband will receive an intimate knowing of one another that you have with no one else. This special secret between just the two of you will bring an incredible depth to your relationship.

God Declares: "I Gave the Gift of Sex for Pleasure."
To hear some Christians talk, you'd think that enjoying sex was like stepping into a tiny rain puddle—there is barely enough water to cover your

big toe. If you've read your Bible, you know God has given no puny puddle of pleasure. His Gift of sex offers us enjoyment equal to the depth of an ocean.

Did you know God's holy Word talks about breasts in a sexual way? If you don't believe this is in the Bible, read Proverbs 5:19. It says: "Let her breasts satisfy you at all times; be exhilarated always with her love."

In the original Hebrew language, the words are even stronger! Linda's husband, who is a theologian, says a very accurate translation of this passage is:

> Let your love and your sexual embrace with your wife intoxicate
> you continually with delight. Always enjoy the ecstasy of her love.

As writers, we are always searching for just the right word to communicate what we are trying to say. We clicked through our entire computer thesaurus and were unable to come up with stronger words for pleasure than *intoxicate* and *ecstasy.* You've seen people who were intoxicated. What happens to them?

• They lose all inhibition.
• Relaxation flows.
• Laughter abounds.
• They think differently.
• They walk and talk differently.

When people are intoxicated, the alcohol *overtakes* them.

God's Word says that after the Gift Exchange on your wedding night, you are to intoxicate your husband with such ocean depths of pleasure that he will be out of control, completely *overtaken* by your sexual love. And, oh yes, *you* are to be *overtaken* by his sexual love too!

God's Word says far more about His Gift being given for pleasure than for the other five reasons put together. God cared so much that you grasp the idea of exquisite pleasure that He included an entire book in the Bible that tells of the joys of sexual love, the Song of Solomon. God says *wait,* but He also clearly says that *His Gift is worth the wait.*

God Declares: "I Gave the Gift of Sex as a Deterrent to Temptation."
God's Gift of sexual passion can be used as a powerful force for good or
for evil. To make certain that His Gift was used for good, our wise God
wrapped His Gift in the bonds of marriage. Proverbs 5 strongly warns a
young man (and young woman) to flee sexual temptation. "Keep your
way far from her and do not go near the door of her house."4 In other
words: "If someone tempts you sexually, get out faster than you can press
the escape key on your computer."

God Declares: "I Gave the Gift of Sex for Comfort."
Does this reason surprise you? It surprised us, yet how tenderly creative
of our God to design the sexual union as a place of comfort. We see an
example of this in 2 Samuel after David and Bathsheba's son has died.
While grieving, "David comforted Bathsheba his wife, and went in to her
and lay with her" (2 Samuel 12:24, NKJV).

Over the lifetime of a marriage, every couple experiences seasons of
deep despair, profound grief, or intense stress. How creative of God to
design a way for a husband and wife to tenderly and compassionately
comfort one another during these difficult times.

God was incredibly ingenious in his blueprint for sexual intimacy.
Through our lovemaking we can create life; experience deep intimacy,
unique knowledge, and exquisite pleasure; and even comfort each other in
times of stress or sorrow.

GOD'S PORTRAIT OF A BRIDE

As you read God's six reasons for sex, did you notice that two keywords
were repeated over and over? In case you missed them, let us point them
out—*husband* and *wife*. The intoxication, the exquisite pleasure, and the
deep intimacy is reserved exclusively for marriage. It is for this reason that
God uses a young bride to picture the abandoned joy of sexual love in
marriage.

When a bride sees sexual intimacy through God's eyes, she understands the holy beauty of sex. Sexual oneness with her husband is a glorious picture of the spiritual oneness Christ longs to have with each believer.

In the sexual relationship, intimacy produces ecstasy—abandoned joy.

In the spiritual relationship, intimacy produces ecstasy—joy unspeakable.[5]

Solomon's bride, as portrayed in the Song of Solomon, lived out "abandoned joy" with her husband. As you read her words, remember that the Song of Solomon was written as poetry, but her message comes through loud and clear, even through the poetry.

Let's look at three specific ways she expressed this abandoned joy.

1. She was free to give in to her sexual desire. The bride reveled in the fact that "My beloved is mine, and I am his" (2:16). She goes on to say, "I am my beloved's, and his desire is for me" (7:10).

2. She was free to be verbally expressive. The young bride was not afraid to make her wishes known. In very specific terms, she gave Solomon lessons in how to touch her body. "Let his left hand be under my head and his right hand embrace me" (2:6).

3. She was free to be adventurous. Within the passionate pages of the Song of Solomon, we see the bride inviting her husband for a getaway in the mountains. With enticing words, she paints a picture of how they will arise early one morning and go to the countryside and make love among the vineyards (7:11-13). Did you know that an outdoor lovemaking escapade was in the Bible?

Few brides jump into the depths of abandoned joy like Solomon's bride. How was she able to be so free and adventurous? We think it has much to do with her commitment to remain sexually pure until God's appointed time for her to experience the Gift. Three times the writer of the Song of Solomon gives this admonition:

Do not stir up nor awaken love until it pleases. (2:7; 3:5; 8:4, NKJV)

The Voices

God's voice on sex is drastically different from the world's voice. We asked several single friends, "What messages does the world communicate about sex?" and, "What messages does God communicate about sex?" Here are their answers.

The World's View

- ～ The world sees sex as a form of entertainment or as a way for someone to get something they want. *Julie*
- ～ Sex is seen as a way to feel close to someone else, but really it is a false intimacy because it is not connected to a commitment. *Becca*
- ～ Sex is a "quick fix" to avoid true intimacy. It is not sacred, but something that can be done with anyone whenever the "urge" strikes. *Ginny*

God's View:

- ～ God reserves sex for two people in a marriage. Marital sex is meant to be secure, bonding, pure, and spirit lifting. *Julie*
- ～ God views sex as intimate, good, sacred. It is sacred in that it enables two people to become one and to know each other in ways you cannot know any other person. *Becca*
- ～ God created sex to be the ultimate physical, spiritual, and emotional love-union between a man and woman. Because this union is so sacred, it is only to be expressed within the lifetime commitment of marriage. *Ginny*

The time to awaken love is the wedding night. When the moment came, Solomon's bride knew God had given her permission to immerse herself with abandoned joy in the Gift of sexual passion.

A TIME TO COMMIT

If you are unable to pray this prayer because of guilt or shame from things that have happened in your past, God has a message of hope for you. Keep reading!

God calls *you* not to awaken love until it pleases. If you have said yes to God's call and have saved the Gift, we applaud you. God applauds you. You have stood strong against the world's confusing voices. Know that your faithful, secret choices bring delight to the heart of God. He rejoices over you with singing and says, "Well done, good and faithful daughter."

God calls you to continue in your commitment to save the Gift. He desires for you now, in this moment, to reaffirm your inward intent. Will you pray?

> *My Lord, I quietly kneel before You to thank You*
> *for giving me the strength to chose Your path of purity.*
> *I WILL continue to pursue Your plan for my life.*
> *I need Your strength, O Lord. Daily burn Your truth*
> *into my heart so that if I marry, I might one day*
> *present my body as a Gift to my husband in a way*
> *that will delight him and bring glory to You.*

The next section on "Recapturing the Gift" contains vital information every woman needs to know. Please answer the Checkpoint question to find out why you must keep reading.

Checkpoint

You have just finished reading section 1, "The Gift," which talks about two aspects of the Gift—first, the idea that God created the Gift of sex and gave it to a husband and wife for their enjoyment; second, that God gift-wrapped you and sealed you at birth so you could give the Gift of your body to your husband on your wedding night. What were your thoughts?

We asked two young women this question and received two very different answers.

Molly: I never realized the Bible had so much to say about sex and that God is so FOR sexual passion in marriage. I loved Tira's story. Staying sexually pure has not been easy, but I am more motivated that ever to save the Gift for marriage, because I think for the first time I truly understand that God wants me to wait because He wants the best for me.

Carina: I wanted to rip up every page and throw it in the trash because it made me feel cheap and dirty. I have given away the Gift so many times I can't even remember all of the recipients. I feel like damaged goods. Tira's story depressed me. The idea of being pure on my wedding night is a joke —it will never come true. It's too late for me.

If you are like Molly—pure in body, soul, and mind—you may be tempted to skip the next section, thinking it doesn't apply to you. Don't. Please keep reading because your prayers are desperately needed! Pray for your friends, your sister, for the many young women you know who need this message. Ask God to speak deeply to their hearts and to do a work of redemptive healing in their lives. Pray too about any information God may want you to share with them.

If you are like Carina and have already given the Gift away, you may be thinking, *It's too late for me.* IT'S NOT TOO LATE! Please, open your heart, clear your mind, and turn the page. God has an important message of hope He wants you to hear.

~

Recapturing the Gift

Come, My child.
Come back to Me.
The guilt and shame you feel has separated us
far too long.
I miss you.
There is much I want to give you.
I want to set you free from the pain of
your past.
I want you to have a new beginning
sexually.
I want to heal you. . .mind, soul,
and body.
I want to give you eternal life.

Come, My child.
With Me, a new beginning is always possible.

Chapter 6

"For This He Died"

Two lines of women snaked around the chairs to the back of the church wanting to share their hearts with us after an Intimate Issues conference.

Linda: As Jen handed me her book, she gushed, "I'm getting married in a month. I can hardly wait to apply everything I've learned!"

Next in line was Jen's friend Kate. While Jen's face looked up, filled with joy, Kate's looked down, streaked with tears. What a contrast. Two brides-to-be, one jubilant, the other downcast.

"I'm getting married in two months," Kate sobbed.

"Have you made wrong choices?" I asked. Her head bobbed up and down. "Has your fiancé forgiven you?" Again a bobbing head said yes.

Taking Kate's face in my hands, I looked into her eyes and said:

"It is for this that Jesus died."

Lorraine: While Linda was comforting Kate, I was with Maggie, who was shaking so violently I thought at first she might be having a seizure. I held her tightly to still the tremors. So softly I could barely hear, Maggie struggled just to get the words out, "I've...had...an abortion. I...killed... my own child... How could I do such an evil thing?" The river of her tears wet my blouse as regret streamed out her eyes. "I've never told another Christian woman what I did; I'm too ashamed."

Hugging her, I whispered, "Well, now you've told a Christian woman, and this Christian woman says to you:

'It is for this that Jesus died.'

"Maggie, Maggie, Jesus died for the little sins we commit every day—the hurtful words, the selfish attitudes—but He also died for your abortion. Do you believe this?"

Linda: Next in my line was Laney. Laney didn't—couldn't—talk. She could only point and weep. Opening her copy of *Intimate Issues* to chapter 14, she trembled as she pointed to the words *sexual abuse.* Quietly I asked, "Was it your father?" She nodded. "And did this set you on a path of destruction where you later made wrong sexual choices?" Again, a nod in between sobs. Enveloping this precious young woman in my arms, I held her and rocked back and forth. "Oh, Laney, God weeps with you. I weep with you," I said. "Your pain is so deep. Oh, Laney, I'm so sorry. But listen! God can redeem even this. I have seen Him do it. He can do it for you!"

It is for this that Jesus died.

To all the Kates who have made wrong choices. To all the Maggies who silently shoulder the burden of hidden sin. To all the Laneys who were victims of sexual abuse and who later became promiscuous we say, *Listen. Listen carefully!*

Jesus died for ALL sin.

Do you believe that Jesus died for *your* sin?

GOD'S GIFT OF HIS SON

This book is about God-given gifts, the Gift of sex that God gives to husbands and wives and the Gift of a bride's pure body to her husband on their wedding night. But God has given each of us another gift—the most important gift ever given—the gift of His Son, Jesus, so that we might know forgiveness of our sin and have eternal life.

> For God so loved the world [substitute your name] that he gave his one and only Son, that whoever believes in him shall not perish but have eternal life. (John 3:16, NIV)

What amazing love that God would give so great a gift! The two of us accepted this gift when we in our late teens. Knowing Jesus has changed our lives. We both know we have eternal life, and we know God's forgiveness personally. We can shout from the rooftops, "Our sins are forgiven."

Have you received this gift? Do you believe that Jesus died for your sins and that He has given you eternal life as a gift? Do you know for certain that if you died today that you would go to heaven? If you aren't sure, we have good news for you! You *can* be sure that your sins are forgiven. You *can* be certain that you will spend eternity in heaven. God is a God who redeems, and it is His desire to redeem you.

The biblical word for *redemption* means "to free by paying a ransom."[1] Perhaps the best way to make this definition come alive is to tell one young woman's story.[2]

Sara and Her Father

Sara trembled. This time she had done it. Drunk driving. DUI would forever be pinned to her chest like a scarlet letter. And her dad—she couldn't think about him. The most respected judge in the city now had a daughter who wore DUI.

Sara was scared. After a horrid night spent in jail, today she would be arraigned in court. We'll let Sara tell you about the worst day of her life.

> As I walked into the courtroom, memories of sitting on my father's knee and playing judge flooded my mind. But today was no game. I felt humiliated and ashamed. The smart-aleck Sara was replaced by a more sober version. I realized I could have killed someone. *Oh God, I'm so sorry. God, if You're there, please listen. Please, please, don't let me go before my dad—any judge but him.*
>
> As the robed figure walked to the bench, his pain-filled eyes locked with mine. My father. As the proceedings began, I had an

outlandish thought. *Dad is hugely disappointed in me, but he's still my dad. Maybe he'll give me a break and let me off.* This was not to happen. The gavel banged twice, and I heard the dreaded words, "Guilty as charged." Then my father levied the maximum penalty the law allowed. One thousand dollars. I couldn't look at him. I wanted to disappear.

But then the strangest thing happened. My father stood up, took off his judge's robe, and came to where I stood. Never will I forget his words. "Sara, you have transgressed against the law, and as a righteous judge, I had to declare you guilty. But, Sara, you are my beloved daughter, and because I love you, I want to pay your penalty for you." With those words, he pulled out his checkbook and wrote out a check for a thousand dollars. Handing it to me, he said, "You are free to go."

You and Your Father

Reflect with us on Sara's story:

- Sara's father loved her.
- Because Sara had transgressed against the law, a penalty had to be paid.
- Her father, the righteous judge, paid the penalty his own justice required.
- Sara accepted her father's payment for her transgression.

Do you see the parallel?

You have broken God's laws. Because God is righteous, His justice demands that a penalty be paid for your sin (Romans 3:23). Your heavenly Father loves you. His love for you is so great that He sent His only Son to pay the penalty for your transgression (John 3:16; Romans 6:23). When Jesus declared from the cross, "It is finished," His words meant that the price for your sin had been "paid in full."[3] *He obtained your release and restoration by paying a price.* Your redemption was accomplished:

COMPLETE,
TOTAL,
OVERWHELMING,
MIND-BOGGLING
REDEMPTION

What amazing love!

The Son of Man did not come to be served, but to serve, and to give His life a ransom for many. (Mark 10:45)

You are not your own; you were bought at a price. Therefore honor God with your body. (1 Corinthians 6:19-20, NIV)

If the Son sets you free, you will be free indeed. (John 8:36, NIV)

The redemption that God offers reaches deep into every hidden place, healing guilt over wrong choices, healing hearts and bodies ravaged by abuse. His redemption is so inclusive that no sin falls outside the boundaries of its grasp. "[Jesus] gave his life to free us from every kind of sin, to cleanse us, and to make us his very own people, totally committed to doing what is right" (Titus 2:14, NLT).

Just as Sara had to reach out her hand and accept her father's gift in order to be free, each of us must reach out our hands and personally receive the payment God supplied so that we can be free. If you have not received this gift, will you do so right now? It's really quite simple. Just talk honestly and openly with God. Tell Him that you are sorry for your sin and accept the payment He offered through the gift of His Son. You might pray something like this:

> God says, "You have eternal life as a free gift."

Dear Lord, I've really messed up.
I know I've done many things that displease You,

and I've broken many of Your laws. I am guilty.
But I believe that Jesus loves me
and that He died to pay the penalty for my sin.
Jesus, in this moment, I reach out to You
and receive the payment You offer.
Please forgive me and come into my life to be my Savior.
Begin to make me into the woman You want me to be.

If you prayed this prayer, we rejoice with you. You are forgiven. You have crossed over from death into life.

No more guilt.

No more shame.

You've been set free.

Believe it, for it is so.

It is for YOU that Jesus died.

Chapter 7

Kendall: One Woman's Journal

If Jesus Christ is your Savior, God has forgiven your sin. Christian women tell us all the time, "Yes! I believe God has forgiven my sin." They even give examples of sins they know God has forgiven—cheating on an algebra exam or lying about when they returned a video so they wouldn't have to pay a late fee. They say, "I believe God has forgiven me for my sexual sin." But there is a problem. Though they speak the words with their lips, forgiveness is not lived out in their lives. Guilt follows them around like a silent shadow.

Why don't these women experience the forgiveness they profess? Why do feelings of guilt continue to haunt them? Because they suspect that sexual sin is different from other sins, and because it is different, it must require additional penance before they can be forgiven.

This was Kendall's problem.

Kendall was a "good girl" who wanted to be a missionary. Perhaps that's why the guilt of her sin ran so deep. Kendall[1] is our friend, and she gave us permission to include part of her journal in this book. She told us, "I think if other women can see what I went through, it will help them." We pray that her words will speak to you.

April 5
Why? Why did I do it? Why God? I wanted more than anything
to be a virgin on my wedding night. Now I've given that away.
Why didn't I say "NO" and just leave? Why did I go to his apartment when I knew we'd be alone?

I know why. I longed for him to touch me. I ached to feel his body next to mine. And while my words were saying, "No," my body was screaming, "Yes." I just didn't think "it" would happen. Oh God, how could something that felt so incredible two hours ago make me feel so wretched now?

April 7
God, please don't hate me. I know what I did was wrong. I heard Your quiet voice telling me to stop when we were going too far, but I ignored it and gave into my passion. I am so weak. Please forgive me. Help me to be strong. Jake and I talked, and we've both agreed: NO MORE SEX until we are married. HELP US, GOD!

May 5
We lasted a month. It seems impossible to go back to kissing after what we did. We really tried, but the pull was like nothing I've ever known. Every time Jake and I were together, his eyes begged for intimacy. Probably mine were sending the same message. God, what do we do? HELP!

October 7
I miss you, God, but I'm too ashamed to talk with You.

November 14
Jake and I had another huge fight today. This time we argued over whether a purple pencil was his or mine. A pencil! What is happening to us? There is so much tension between us. Tonight we talked about breaking up. I was so sure we'd spend the rest of our lives together. Now I can't stand the thought of spending the whole day with him. What is going on? I'm so confused.

November 18
Jake's been pretty chummy lately with his lab partner, Alyssa. Does he want to start seeing her? He's been a real jerk all week. Part of

me says, "Go ahead. Get out of my life so I can get on with mine."
But another part is in anguish over the thought of calling it quits. I
feel "tied" to him because I let him have the most intimate part of
me. If Jake goes, a part of me will go with him. God, oh, God,
what have I done? What should I do now?

December 30
I don't think I'll ever stop crying. How can I live without Jake? But
how can I live with this continual guilt?

January 9
It is over. I want to go home. I don't want to be here—I don't feel
like doing anything. I hate my life. I hate myself. I can't find God.
I wish I could go to sleep and never wake up.

During the next eight months, Kendall rode a roller coaster of
emotions—loneliness, guilt, anger. Feelings of depression constantly
threatened to engulf her. Eventually the pain subsided, and she began to
move on with her life. She graduated from college and got an excellent job
in advertising. Now we pick up her journal again, four years later.

July 7
Finally, Casey proposed. Of course I said yes! God, how can I ever
thank You for giving me this man who loves You as much as he
loves me and who forgives me. I know he's forgiven me—but there
is this dark cloud hanging over me—my past. What I would give
to be a virgin again! I wish I'd never known another man's body.
Oh God, I wish I could go back.

January 1
A new year. We had a ball last night with our friends, laughing
about the silly things that happened last year and sharing our hopes
for this year. My hopes for this year are pretty obvious—a great
wedding for one! And that I will be the perfect wife for Casey. He is

so tender with me. When he walked me to my door after the party, neither of us could bear to be apart. But he knew and I knew that to walk in that apartment and give us the luxury of being alone would be inviting temptation! So he grabbed my hand and said, "Come share a piece of pie with me at the Village Inn." We talked for three more hours before he kissed me good-bye at my door. Oh, for the day when we won't have to say good-bye.

February 1
Two more weeks! The girls at the office threw a lingerie party for me, and I got some pretty racy stuff! The party was fun—I just wish the cloud of "if only's" would go away. I ate too much cake. Better do a double workout on the abs tomorrow, or I won't even fit into my new teddy…

February 2
Spent two hours finalizing honeymoon details with Casey. Feelings of guilt hovered. I feel guilty that I will be his "first," but he won't be mine. God, please, please erase the images in my mind, the pictures that won't go away.

February 12
Two more days and I'll be Mrs. Casey Austin. A Valentine Day's wedding, I'm so excited! I feel like a princess in my dress and the bridesmaids all in red velvet. I have my vows memorized. The cake is spectacular. Relatives are beginning to arrive. Everything is set. I finally decided on the black, lacy teddy for our first night because I think it's the one Casey would like the most. God, please help me not to dwell on the past. *I feel scared and unworthy.*

Linda: Five years after her wedding, Kendall was the mommy of two little boys and very concerned about her unexciting sexual relationship with her husband. She had just finished reading *Intimate Issues* and came to me in tears.

"Linda, now that it's okay to have sex, why don't I want to? I just didn't think it would be like this."

As Kendall poured out her heart, I could feel her guilt, so I asked, "Is it possible that you do not give yourself permission to enjoy sex because you are trying to prove to God how sorry you are for what you did? Also, you said 'pictures' of things from your past still come to mind. Maybe you don't want Casey to touch you in certain ways because it reminds you of things you did with Jake."

I told her about the Gift Exchange[2] and asked, "Have you ever given your body to Casey as a gift?" She got very quiet.

"No, I think I've always withheld a part of myself," she replied sheepishly.

"What do you think God would want you to do?"

Her creative answer took me totally by surprise. "Our anniversary is on Valentine Day next month, and I can't think of a better gift to give him than me."

Was her gift to Casey a hit? Let's return to the pages of Kendall's journal and find out.

February 14
Today is our anniversary. This evening I will give my body to Casey as a gift. I am so nervous. Why? This is what You desire of me, God. Why am I so nervous?

February 15
Last night I told Casey that on our wedding night I had not fully given my body to him. Over the years there had always been lots of "ifs and noes." Depending on my mood, I would give a little of my body or all of my body, but always it was MY decision for it was MY body. So with a bow on and nothing else, I stood before him and offered myself to him. He wept.

Do I feel different? Yes. It was like being a virgin again because I truly gave myself for the first time.

Kendall's actions beautifully illustrate the Gift Exchange that God desires for every husband and wife. But it took Kendall many years before she could fully give herself to Casey because she was not able to live out the forgiveness God offered. She lived with guilt as a single and also as a wife.

God says, "You can have a new beginning sexually."

Kendall does not want this to be your story. Neither do we. So please turn the page and discover how you can break the ties of your sexual past.

Chapter 8

The Ties of Sexual Sin

Kendall wanted to save the Gift until marriage. When she failed, she asked God to forgive her. She made a commitment—NO MORE SEX. But despite her intentions, she once again found herself physically entangled with Jake. Again she sought forgiveness, and though intellectually she believed God HAD forgiven her, guilt clung to her like Saran Wrap.

Kendall's story raises some good questions:

- Why was it so difficult for her and Jake to stop having sex?
- Why was it so hard for her to get over Jake after they broke up?
- Why did she still feel "tied" to him years later?
- Why did she continue to think about Jake even after she was married?
- Why did she continue to feel guilty even though God had forgiven her?

When we talked to Kendall, she told us: "I always felt that there was something about my sexual sin that made it different from other sins I had committed. I believed that this sin was a worse sin than telling a lie or gossiping about a friend, and so I felt I had to go through some sort of special punishment before God could really forgive me."

Kendall's thinking is common among the women we talk with. But is her thinking right? Is it biblical?

According to Scripture, Kendall's premise is correct—sexual sin IS different from other sin. But her conclusion is wrong. Because of the finished work of Christ on the cross, God forgives all sin—including sexual sin. No exceptions. Kendall could do NOTHING that would have made her sin more forgivable in God's eyes because it was already marked "paid in full."

If Kendall had understood the nature of sexual sin, it is possible she could have appropriated God's forgiveness sooner and been spared the lingering feelings of guilt.

What we are about to share with you is vital. It is information Kendall wishes she'd had; it is something we wish we had known in our dating years. This concept is not often talked about, nor is it widely understood. We pray that as we look into God's Word, His Spirit will speak to you about the true nature of sexual sin.

THE NATURE OF SEXUAL SIN

Flee from sexual immorality. All other sins a man commits are outside his body, but he who sins sexually sins against his own body.
(1 Corinthians 6:18, NIV)

In this verse Paul lumps together "all other sins" as sins committed "outside the body." Then he holds up sexual sin and says, in effect: "Look! *Sexual sin is different.* Unlike other sin, sexual sin is a sin against your own body."

Because sexual sin is not like other sins, it affects us differently. To understand how it affects us, we need to go back to the beginning, back to God's original purpose and design for sexual intimacy.

In the garden the Lord created one man and one woman. Separately, they brought glory to the Almighty, but *together* they reflected His image. So God fashioned a Gift for the man and the woman, and He wove into the intrinsic nature of the Gift a profound mystery. God's Gift was holy, for in the intertwining of their bodies, in the melting together in intense pleasure, a miracle happened: Two separate beings became one, tied together in body, soul, and spirit.

When God's Gift is shared between a husband and wife, these ties are exquisite ribbons of beauty and passion, safe cords that bind the couple together when outside forces threaten to pull them apart. But when two people misuse God's Gift, and soul ties develop *outside* the bond of marriage, they can become ropes that bind and chaff, tying a woman to a man even when he is no longer part of her life.

Why was it so hard for Kendall to stop having sex with Jake? Because through sexual intimacy, she and Jake had became one, tied together in body, soul, and spirit.

Why was it so difficult for Kendall after she and Jake broke up? Because they were one. When he walked away, Kendall literally felt ripped apart.

Why did Kendall continue to think about Jake after she got married? Because even though she had not seen him for years, she still had soul ties to him.

Why did Kendall continue to feel guilty even though she believed—intellectually—that God had forgiven her? Because what was in her head did not seep down into her heart. She felt there was something else she had to do for God to truly forgive her.

Many women struggle to embrace God's forgiveness for sexual sin. For some, the soul ties snap the moment they pray for forgiveness; they immediately embrace the freedom they have in Christ. For others (like Kendall), the tie tugs at them over the years until God speaks fresh truth to them and they are able to embrace His forgiveness. For still others, the soul ties are so pervasive that they become a tangled, unmanageable mess. If these ties are not broken and the pattern of behavior is not changed, the consequences of sin can prove devastating, not only in the life of the woman, but also in the lives of those she loves.

CONSEQUENCES OF SEXUAL SIN

Sexual sin is never without consequence.

> Do not be deceived: God cannot be mocked. A man reaps what he
> sows. The one who sows to please his sinful nature, from that

nature will reap destruction; the one who sows to please the Spirit, from the Spirit will reap eternal life. (Galatians 6:7-8, NIV)

If you sow sexual sin, you will reap sexual consequences. Some women experience them immediately, but most don't come face to face with the consequences until years later.

Kendall's consequence was lingering guilt. For others, it might be

• living with herpes, AIDS, or another sexual disease
• confessing your sin to the man you marry
• someday telling your daughter about your past
• waiting until heaven to meet the child you aborted
• fighting a war in your mind with the sexual images stored there
• a strained relationship with God because of your shame
• not feeling whole as a woman because you have separated your spirituality from your sexuality

Different consequences impact women in different measure. Some consequences are obvious. Others, like separating spirituality and sexuality, require more explanation. Let's look at this consequence in greater depth.

SEPARATING SPIRITUALITY AND SEXUALITY

Darcy was a Bible study leader and a highly respected member of her church, but from the moment we met her, we sensed something was amiss in her life. We knew that Darcy was a district sales manager for a national company and that she was an avid rock climber, but we later learned something else—something she had told no one. For the past four years, Darcy had been enmeshed in a sexual relationship with another woman in her Bible study.

After confessing her sin to us, she begged, "Please, don't say I have to stop teaching the Bible study. I really want to serve the Lord."

Darcy truly loved God. How was it possible for her to serve Him while simultaneously being involved in an illicit lesbian relationship? By separating her spirituality from her sexuality. She put her spirituality in one compartment, her sexuality in another, and erected a wall between the two. When she was with her lover, she operated out of her sexual compartment, but when she was at church, she operated out of her spiritual compartment. When we met Darcy, the wall between her sexuality and spirituality had begun to crack, and she was racked with guilt.

Darcy described her guilt-soaked heart with these words.

> The wall I had erected between my spirituality and my sexuality protected me from guilt and conviction—but it also prevented my escape. The existence I had crafted became my tomb, a tomb for a hardened heart. It hadn't begun that way, but at some point what I'd created to control my sin now controlled me. I cried out to God and pleaded for Him to show me a way out of the tomb of my own making. God heard my cry. He made the way of escape by sending the two of you to convict me of my sin. The wall came tumbling down. Hallelujah!

As we prayed through a prayer of forgiveness with Darcy, she made a covenant with God that she would cut the soul ties with the friend who had been her sexual partner. She confessed her sin and embraced the forgiveness God offered. God forgave her, but her actions still had some difficult consequences. As a sign of her repentance and to help her stick with her commitment to be sexually pure, she agreed to do the following:

- eliminate all contact with the woman who had been her sexual partner
- confess her sin to her pastor and agree to take a sabbatical from teaching and not return until God and the pastor agreed the time was right
- tell her Bible study group that she was temporarily resigning as the leader until God showed her it was right for her to return

All three actions required tremendous courage and God's enabling strength, but Darcy was faithful and so was her Lord. For the next five years God did a deep healing in Darcy's heart. Her pastor recently gave permission for her to return to teaching. The Lord also brought a godly man into her life, and he asked her to marry him. She wrote us this e-mail:

> When I told Paul about my past, he broke down in tears. I cried too as I stood at the center of my pool of sin and watched the rings circle out from me and create pain in so many people. Even still, the Lord continues to fill me up with HIMSELF! And now He has blessed me with Paul. How grateful I am that the walls between my sexuality and my spirituality have crumbled. I am a whole woman, and I am excited to become Paul's wife. God is gracious. I have no words to thank Him.

We have a great God who loves us and has the power to redeem our hearts and our sinful actions. What an awesome truth: *God can cut your soul ties and restore sexual wholeness.*

In the next chapter we want to take you into the pages of Scripture and introduce you to another woman who beautifully demonstrates the depth of God's forgiveness of sexual sin.

Why Wait?

INSIGHT FROM SOME WHO WAITED AND MANY WHO DIDN'T

At an Intimate Issues conference we asked several hundred married women these questions: Did you wait to have sex until you were married? If so, are you glad? If not, what would you say to single women about your decision? More than 90 percent had NOT waited. Without exception, they regretted their decision. Of the 10 percent who had waited, all said they were glad they did. Here are some of their comments.

- Every time I had sex, I took a piece of myself and gave it away. By the time I got married, there wasn't much of me left to give. God is working to bring me back to wholeness. Please, please don't give yourself away bit by bit through sexual touching. You will rob yourself and your future husband of what God wants you to have.

- As a teen I considered myself overweight and shy. I felt unaccepted, and I was willing to do whatever it took to be accepted, to be popular. When I was seventeen, I got pregnant. I kept the baby and years later married another man, but because of my promiscuous behavior, there is not much intimacy in our marriage.

- Thirteen years ago I got pregnant and then had an abortion, which still haunts me and makes me feel unworthy of God's love. I kept it all a secret, just like the secret that I was wrongly introduced to sex at an early age through incest with my father. I've been to counseling and I am learning: Don't keep secrets. I am now married and have three daughters. I will encourage my daughters to wait for sex until marriage.

～ My husband and I waited, but during our engagement we were often alone, which led to intense kissing, arousals, and petting. I regret this, as does my husband. I would caution engaged women that engagement does not give you an excuse to "rattle" the Gift and tear away part of the wrappings because you know that you will get to open it soon.

～ I waited because it is who I am… God brought me a wonderful, godly man. I'm glad I waited because my husband was pleased, but most of all I'm glad I waited to please my God.

～ I believed the lie that I needed to have sex before marriage in order to fit in with others or to be loved by someone. This caused me much heartache and held me in bondage. Sex before marriage put a bond between Satan and me and a wall between God and me.

～ I didn't wait, and I regret it. I am more special than I gave myself or God credit for!

～ I wish I had waited. God has now set me free, but for a LONG TIME I struggled with images and pictures—I wouldn't let my husband touch me in certain ways because it reminded me of how my boyfriend had touched me. Praise God for the new freedom I now have with my husband, but I wish, so wish that on my honeymoon night I could have given my husband this beautiful body without fingerprints all over it.

～ I never had sexual intercourse before marriage, but I regret getting involved with oral sex with my fiancé (we broke up before we were married) and then my husband when we were engaged. My actions hindered me spiritually, emotionally, and sexually in my marriage.

Chapter 9

Cutting the Ties of Sexual Sin

Now one of the Pharisees invited Jesus to have dinner with him, so he went to the Pharisee's house and reclined at the table. When a woman who had lived a sinful life in that town learned that Jesus was eating at the Pharisee's house, she brought an alabaster jar of perfume, and as she stood behind him at his feet weeping, she began to *wet his feet* with her tears. Then she *wiped them* with her hair, *kissed them* and *poured perfume on them.* (Luke 7:36-38, NIV, emphasis added)

The woman described in Luke's gospel had a name, but the Bible does not record it. She is called merely the "sinful woman."[1]

THE SINFUL WOMAN

We are not told how this woman lost her virginity. Perhaps she gave her body willingly to some young man in a moment of youthful passion, or perhaps her virginity was taken from her by force. Either way, the moment she lost her virginity, she lost her value, because in those days a groom's family paid a bride price for a bride—but only if she was a virgin.

Though no man would pay her bride price, this woman found other ways to make men pay. For a few coins, she joined herself with them. The first time she probably did not notice the tie that bound her to him—at least, not until he left and a part of her went with him. Then there was another man and another tie. Then another…and another…and another. At the point in Scripture where we meet her, the ties of sexual sin are so binding that you can almost hear her scream: "I hate my life. I hate what men have done to me, and what I have done to myself. I want out! Jehovah, if You are there, if You are listening, please, please deliver me from this hell."

But God seemed not to hear, and day after day the men still came, not to see her, but to use her body.

Then she learned that Jesus was in town and that He was having dinner at the Pharisee's house. She knew about Jesus. He was a miracle worker, a healer. He was a holy man, yet He ate with sinners. If anyone could help her, it would be this Jesus.

So she reached for her finest cloak and raced down the cobblestone streets that led to Simon's home.

Somehow she got past the servant at the door and slipped into the shadows of the large room lit by oil lamps. In the center of the room, prominent men of the town reclined around a large, low table, enjoying a meal. At the place of honor, next to Simon, was Jesus.

She walked over and stood behind Him. Goodness radiated from Him. The light of holiness seemed to surround Him, exposing her own sinfulness. One part of her wanted to run and hide, but another part knew that He was her only hope. But why would He want to help her, a wicked sinner?

She hung her head in shame. A tear slipped down her cheek. Then another. Suddenly the floodgates opened, and she fell to the floor, weeping. Her tears formed tiny rivulets through the red dust on Jesus' feet.[2] Each tear carried a confession. Each confession had a name. Each name was a man. Each man exposed a tie. "Forgive me for Jacob. Forgive me for Samuel. Forgive me for the man with the scar on his cheek whose name I never knew."

On and on she sobbed until all of the sorrow and regret of the years had been released, until there were no more faces, no more tears, no more ties. She was spent, her cauldron of agony empty. Then, as if coming out of a trance, she suddenly realized the mess she'd made of Jesus' feet! Embarrassed, she looked for a towel to dry them, but seeing none, she released the clasp that held her hair, and waves of liquid silk spilled over her shoulders.

Gently, tenderly, she wiped Jesus' feet with her hair. Peace slowly curled around her, and she felt its firm grip. Her anguish was gone. In that moment she knew that God had wiped away her sin.

The corners of her mouth curled into a smile. Pressing her warm lips against his damp skin, she kissed his feet over and over and over. "Jesus, oh, Jesus. You have set me free. You have made me new. How can I ever thank You?"

Then she remembered the flask of perfume tucked inside her cloak. This was her scent, applied before encounters with her lovers. She would no longer need it for that purpose. Retrieving the flask, she broke open the seal and, in an act of worship, poured out the fragrance upon Jesus' feet. Her scent mingled with His, and fragrant fields of heather engulfed them in sweetness.

The ties of her past were no more, but in her worship a new tie had formed—a tie that would forever connect her with the Lover of her soul.

Jesus lifted the woman's chin and looked deeply into her eyes. With the authority of Jehovah He proclaimed what she already knew: "Your sins are forgiven" (Luke 7:48, NIV).

God says, "You can be free from guilt and shame."

A NEW BEGINNING

The woman who left Simon's house that evening was no longer "the sinful woman" but a new woman with a new heart. A new soul. A new mind. AND a new body. She was a new creation with a new ability to live a life of holiness and purity.

What Jesus did for this woman He can do for you.

What is your sin? Is it a mind full of garbage—pornographic images or dirty jokes? Have you engaged in intimate touching or sexual intercourse with another person? Have you had an abortion? An affair with a married man? Done something too horrible to put into words?

Please, please hear us. No matter how awful your sin, regardless of what you have done,

It is for this that Jesus died.

Jesus stands ready to forgive you. He doesn't want you to have "head knowledge" forgiveness where you say, "Oh, I know God has forgiven me," but deep down, well-springing, spilling-forth, overflowing forgiveness that causes you to wildly spin around in joy, freedom, and gratitude.

He invites you now to kneel at His feet and go through the same four life-transforming steps you just witnessed.

1. Wet His feet with your tears. Confess your sin. Pray:

> *Jesus, I know it hurt You when I committed sexual sin*
> *by _____ (name the offense)*
> *with _____ (name the person).*
> *I understand that through this sexual act I joined my soul*
> *with _____'s. Please forgive me for (offense)*
> *and break all ties that occurred in that moment.*
> *Return to me the part of myself I gave away*
> *and make me whole. Close forever the door*
> *of sinful thought and action toward _____.*

Pray this prayer and name every act, every person God brings to mind.

2. Wipe His feet with your hair. Believe that God has wiped away your sin. Pray:

> *Lord, You have said that You have wiped away my sin,*
> *that it is gone forever. By faith I believe: "It is finished."*

3. Kiss His feet with gratitude. Thank Him for what He has done. Pray:

Thank You, thank You, Jesus. Thank You for dying for me.
Thank You for setting me free. Thank You that I am new.

4. *Pour perfume upon His feet.* Worship the Lover of your soul. Pray:

Oh Jesus, I worship You. May my worship
be a sweet fragrance to You.

When Jesus forgives your sin, you become new. You have a new heart. A new soul. A new mind. AND a new body. The forgiveness He offers is complete. How complete is it? Turn the page and find out!

Sexual Sins of the Heart

God specifically says that sexual sin includes not only sins of the body but also sins of the heart and tongue. God's standard for purity is higher than man's standard. In Jesus' day, people viewed adultery as a sin committed in the body, but Jesus said that if you look at another person with lust in your heart, you commit adultery (Matthew 5:27-28). Here are some other standards for sexual purity from God's Word.

"Let no unwholesome word proceed from your mouth" (Ephesians 4:29). The Greek word is very descriptive and literally means "dirty rotten garbage."[3]

"It is shameful even to talk about the things that ungodly people do in secret." (Ephesians 5:12, NLT)

"Let there be no sexual immorality, impurity, or greed among you. Such sins have no place among God's people. Obscene stories, foolish talk, and coarse jokes—these are not for you. Instead, let there be thankfulness to God." (Ephesians 5:3-4, NLT)

Chapter 10

Can I Become a Virgin Again?

We asked ten young women, "Is it possible to become a virgin again?" After the stares, glares, and gulps subsided, they gave us these answers.

"I wish."

"Why not ask, 'Can I relive last summer?'"

"It sounds impossible."

Yes, it does sound impossible, but "nothing is impossible with God" (Luke 1:37, NIV).

Once a man asked Jesus a "sounds impossible" question. Nicodemus was a ruler of the Jews who secretly came to Jesus at night. When Jesus made the astounding statement to him that in order to have eternal life, a person had to be born again, Nicodemus became very confused and asked, "How can a man be born when he is old? Surely he cannot enter a second time into his mother's womb to be born!" (John 3:1-4, NIV). Jesus answered by talking about a second birth, a spiritual birth. "Flesh gives birth to flesh, but the Spirit gives birth to spirit" (John 3:6, NIV).

Just as a person cannot climb back into a mother's womb and literally be born physically again, no one can reconnect the torn tissue and become a *physical* virgin again. But just as Nicodemus experienced a spiritual birth that led to eternal life, a person can experience a spiritual "rebirth" of purity. *Spiritually*, a man or woman can become "virginal."

The word *virgin* means to be pure and chaste. One definition of virginity is: "Freedom for consecration to the Lord; it means not only bodily purity, but essentially the will of the heart to belong more completely to Christ and to be available for his service."[1] Our friend, beginning today you can become as a virgin in body, mind, and soul.

Do we hear you saying, "Okay, Linda and Lorraine, first you say becoming a virgin again sounds impossible, then you say I can become *as a virgin*. Is that the same thing? Can I become a virgin again or not?"

Well, yes you can.

Well, no you can't.

Confused? How can the answer be both yes and no?

Physically, the answer is no, because there is never another first time to open the Gift. The initial wrapping God has placed in a woman's body can only be removed once. But spiritually, the answer is yes, because God makes it *very* possible to start all over again.

A second chance spiritually means there are no limitations to what you can become. The God who made the universe out of nothing can take the raw material of your past and make from it something beautiful.[2] He is the God who specializes in bringing beauty out of ashes. If you knelt at the feet of Jesus and asked forgiveness for your past sexual sin, believe His promise. *Your past is in the past.* Now it is time to commit your present and your future to Him.

A TIME TO COMMIT

The word *commit* means to "bind by a pledge."[3] If you have unbound the soul ties of your past, you are then ready to bind yourself to God and His way of purity. Psalm 119:30 says, "I have chosen the faithful way." We urge you to make a commitment that from this day forward you will be as a virgin in thought, word, and deed.

To do this, express to God your own prayer of commitment or say something like this:

> *My Lord, You have forgiven me and made me as a virgin*
> *again. Now I commit from this day forward that by Your*

grace I will live as a virgin in thought, word, and deed.
Thank You that I can now look forward to my wedding day,
when I will give the Gift of my body to my husband.

This is a life-altering prayer. Mark this day on your heart and seal it in your mind. Here are some possible ways to do this:

- Write out your commitment on a nice piece of paper and keep it in your Bible or put it in a pretty box on your nightstand.
- Buy a journal and write your prayer of commitment on the first page. Then continue writing in your journal about the ways God leads you on His path of purity.
- Write today's date in your Bible next to Psalm 119:30: "I have chosen the faithful way."

Congratulations! You are on a new path, one of joy, freedom, and newness. But as we have said, while true commitment to purity can make you as a virgin again, if you have given away the Gift, there will still be consequences for your wrong choices. One consequence you may one day face is telling your boyfriend about your sexual past. How do you do this?

TELLING YOUR BOYFRIEND ABOUT YOUR PAST

First, keep quiet about your sexual past unless you are discussing marriage. Every guy you date does NOT need this information. But if you are in a serious relationship, and God has revealed to you that you need to be honest with your boyfriend, what should you say? How do you say it?

Scenario One. If you are not a virgin physically, you might say something like this:

> I need to tell you something important. I am not a virgin physically. I wish that I could go back and make different choices. But God has forgiven me, and I pray you can also forgive me. For the past (one year, six months—whatever the time has been) I have been walking God's path, and I am totally committed to continue

to walk only God's way. I know that He has made me pure again, and I hold this purity with a firm grip until my wedding night.

Scenario Two. If you are still technically a virgin, but you know you are not pure because you have done everything *except* cross the intercourse barrier, you might say something like this:

I need to tell you something important. Although I am still a virgin, I've made some wrong sexual choices that I deeply regret. God has forgiven me, and I pray you can also forgive me. For the past (one year, six months—whatever the time has been) I have been walking God's path, and I am totally committed to continue to walk only God's way. I hold my purity with a firm grip and will continue to save it until my wedding night.

These are just suggestions; the most important thing is that you be honest and that you stress:

Who you are *now.*

Where you are headed *now.*

DO NOT stress where you've been.

God says, "You can become as a virgin again."

What you say doesn't need to be polished and perfect—just share your heart. This is what Cheri did. Her boyfriend, Jeremy, was a godly twenty-five-year-old virgin committed to waiting (a rare commodity). Cheri had a past and feared that when Jeremy learned of it, he would walk out the door…forever. Here is what happened the night she told him about her past.

Jeremy watched while I frantically paced the floor. I couldn't bear to tell him, to break his heart. He had kept himself pure, and he assumed I had too. He had no clue about the terrible things that I'd done.

He took me by the shoulders and said, "Cheri, it's okay! Whatever is bothering you, you can tell me about it." But I couldn't get the words out; I didn't know how to tell him about the horrible things I'd done. Finally I just spit it out, "Jeremy, not only am I not a virgin, but a year ago I had an abortion."

Jeremy got real quiet, too quiet. I wanted to tell him about my commitment to purity, but he looked so stunned I couldn't say anything. Did he hate me? Would he say he never wanted to see me again? After a pause that seemed like eternity, he looked into my eyes and said the most incredible words ever spoken, "Will you marry me?"

Perhaps not every boyfriend/fiancé will forgive just as Jeremy did. But we know one Man who has. The Lord Jesus looks at your sin, takes your hands in His, looks deeply into your eyes, and says, "Will you be my spiritual bride?"

White Dress Guilt

My fiancé was a virgin, I was not. I remember sobbing to a girlfriend as I showed her my white wedding dress. I didn't deserve to wear white. I felt like I was giving him garbage. How could he love me? How could he want me? I'll never forget what she said:

"Jordan, when you invited Christ into your heart and asked His forgiveness for all of your sins, He made you like a virgin again. You get to start all over. It will be like you're a virgin on your wedding night. It may even hurt."

It did.

Chapter 11

Natalie: One Woman's Healing

I pray
that you,
being rooted and established in love,
may have power to grasp
how wide
and long
and high
and deep
is the
love of God.[1]

Kendall and Darcy journeyed deeper into God's love as they embraced His forgiveness. The sinful woman experienced the depth of God's love for her when Jesus forgave her sins. As you prayed through your own life and received forgiveness, we hope that you, too, began to grasp the depth of God's love for you.

But perhaps the issue for you is not a sin you committed—you were an innocent victim of someone else's sin. If this is your situation, we weep with you. God weeps with you. He NEVER intended that His beautiful Gift should be used in such a vile way.

Today, right now, God wants to give you hope. He wants to heal you and make you new again. We know He can do this for you because we have personally seen Him bring newness to many abused women.

The story that follows is true. It is a glorious story of the extent of

God's redemptive healing. BUT it is also heartbreaking, and we would ask you to ask God if He would have you read it.

We are leaving out many of the details because they would hurt your heart. The evil done to Natalie was not far removed from the horrors of the many Nazi concentration camps of Adolf Hitler's regime. Natalie's Auschwitz was within her soul. And she was sent to this prison of pain not by a mad dictator but by her own mother and father.

We'll let Natalie tell you her story.[2]

The man and woman who gave me my genetic makeup were Judy and Don. I can't call them mother and father because they were never that to me. Judy, my birth-woman person, dressed my sisters and me up for church each Sunday and paraded us down the church aisle like trained monkeys to the front row, where we were expected to sit quietly "on display." This charade was repeated at least twice every week, and I would hear about this God and His Son, Jesus, and how They loved me.

Judy and Don were pillars of our small church. She played the organ, and he was an elder. They were also respected members in the community. To get a bank loan, Don needed only a handshake.

On the outside we looked like a very good, loving, kind, and honorable family. But the smiles were pasted on and the hugs were fake. All were part of a façade necessary to hide the horror underneath.

In reality, Don, the church elder, was a warlock, and Judy, the church organist, was a witch. They forced my sisters and me to participate weekly in their satanic cult, a cult so evil that it defies description.

When I was six months old, like most babies born into satanic cults, I was sacrificed sexually on Satan's altar. This ceremony is the cult's cruel counterpart to a Christian baby dedication, only I was dedicated to father Satan. I won't tell you the details, except to tell you that you could not conjure up in your mind anything so terrible as what really took place. For many years, like other girls in the cult, I was a sex object to be used by men any place, in any way, at any time.

I remember one Sunday when my birth-woman person dressed me up in a pretty white dress with white panties, white socks, and shoes for church. Then, after worship services, she drove me to a secret location where I was paraded around and stripped of my clothing as part of another "worship service." Then I was washed off and re-dressed, and since I hadn't vomited or screamed, I received a rare treat—an ice cream cone.

My body was not my own. I had no rights. I was allowed no opinions and could not object to whatever anyone wanted to do to me. Sadistic punishment awaited my slightest whimper of complaint. As I was told repeatedly, I was an "it," a "thing." Fear and terror were the food and drink of my existence. I survived by crawling down deep inside myself when the despicable sexual evils were done. The real me was gone, and I let some other part of myself perform whatever had to be done in order to survive.

Through some miraculous events, I broke loose of the cult. But I will never feel free as active members hunt down those who leave in order to force them to return. I changed my name and did everything I could to disassociate myself from the terror, but what had been done to me manifested itself in sick ways. I often wore six pairs of underpants as a wall of protection from further violation. I couldn't bring myself to wear a dress because it would allow a man easy access. I hated my femininity, despised men, and walked around in a constant state of fear.

But a little part of me had hope. I think God cupped His hand around a tiny bit of innocence in the heart of that little girl who heard about the love of Jesus as she sat in that church pew, and He told Satan, "You can't have this part." The hope was only a flicker, but I ran to the sliver of Light in that child because it was the only Light in my dark, dark life. I knelt at the flame and pleaded with

God to help me. He did. First He said He wanted to be my Abba Papa, a true Father who loves, protects, and nourishes. Then He sent loving counselors and caring friends who would be His arms and His love to walk with me through my long journey of healing.

Natalie was in the midst of her journey when we met her, and even though she had experienced a lot of healing, the core of her sexuality was still deeply wounded. Natalie's counselors had warned her, "Your sexuality was the first thing taken from you; it will be the last part of you to heal."

As we stood on the stage teaching about the incredible beauty and holiness of God's Gift of sex, Natalie's stomach twisted into knots. Even though it was anguish for her to listen to the truth, she knew she had to. The deep lies rooted in her soul would never be released until God's truth took their place.

Natalie was at the conference because Joe, a caring friend, had signed her up and driven her there. As she squirmed in her seat, Joe sat in his car in the parking lot, praying for Natalie and for us. He understood Natalie's pain for he, too, was one of God's walking wounded.

Joe told us:[3]

> I was severely sexually abused as a small child, and I came into adulthood full of wounds that had festered, causing me to cringe in pain at the slightest criticism or rejection. In my attempt to soothe the ache, I made unhealthy choices of sexual relationships with both men and women.
>
> My inner pain led me to pursue power and position, and I made vast sums of money. From the world's perspective, I had arrived. But emptiness was my constant companion, and I continued to make sexual choices that produced guilt and grief.
>
> But thank God, He never took His hand off me. He was faithful, gentle, and patient with me. I discovered that no matter how many sexual partners, no matter how many unhealthy soul ties, no matter how lost and lonely, no matter how abused physi-

cally, emotionally, or spiritually, THERE IS HOPE, AND THE HOPE IS IN KNOWING JESUS.

Working together as business partners, Natalie and Joe had become good friends. Secretly, Natalie was praying for a loving, tender wife for Joe. Meanwhile, Joe was asking God for a gentle, loving husband for Natalie. Surprise filled their hearts when they realized they were the answers!

But can two very wounded people possibly create a healthy marriage? How could they ever see sex as anything but disgustingly vile? Can a man and woman so scarred by sexual evil ever see sexual passion as a Gift from God?

God says, "You can be healed in mind, soul, and body."

We'll let Natalie tell you. You will rejoice as you read her description of their wedding night.

After the official wedding ceremony, we sat alone together on the couch and shared communion. We prayed vows and commitments before God and to each other—vows for a lifetime. We then prayed for each other. Our oneness started in the spiritual.

Then we invited HIM into our marriage bed. Slowly we undressed each other and took a shower together—literally washing each other in words of love, patience, gentleness, kindness, care, commitment, and prayer.

As we made love, the presence and sweetness of God was like a gentle rain, hovering over us and pouring out His love, pouring out His peace and joy, cleansing and healing, and pouring out His gift of lovemaking for us. We lay in each other's arms, thrilled, in awe of God and HIS GIFT TO US. We felt no shame, no guilt, no ugliness, no pain, no terror, and no fear.

It was the most beautiful moment either of us had ever experienced—not just a physical act of the flesh, it was first spiritual, then emotional, then physical. Amazingly, we both felt like virgins! Only God could give us this miracle.

Why have we told you this story? Because we want you to see the height and depth, the length and breath of God's redemptive power. If He can bring two severely wounded people to the place where they feel "like virgins again," He can bring you to the same place. No wrong choice you have ever made is so wrong that God cannot redeem it. No evil done to you is so evil that God cannot redeem it.

Two years have passed since Natalie and Joe's wedding day. In a recent

Additional Help for Sexual Abuse

Tapes
- "Healing Childhood Traumas," the story of Stephanie Fast. Contact Focus on the Family at (719) 531-3400 and ask for two tapes, CS298.

Books
- Dan B. Allender, *The Wounded Heart* (Colorado Springs: NavPress, 1990). Book and workbook.
- Henry Cloud and John Townsend, *Boundaries: When to Say Yes, When to Say No to Take Control of Your Life* (Grand Rapids: Zondervan, 1992). Book and workbook.
- Jan Frank, *Door of Hope* (Nashville: Nelson, 1995).
- Cynthia Spell Humbert, *Deceived by Shame, Desired by God* (Colorado Springs: NavPress, 2001).
- Harry W. Schaumburg, *False Intimacy: Understanding the Struggle of Sexual Addiction* (Colorado Springs: NavPress, 1992).

Organizations
- Freedom in Christ Ministries, Neil Anderson, 10 West Dry Creek Circle, Littleton, CO 80120; (303) 730-4211.

letter to us, Natalie wrote one of the most hope-filled statements we've ever heard:

The beauty of our intimacy only increases. GOD is restoring what was taken from both of us. I never knew that one could have such peace and such joy as this. It's as vast and as deep as the horror that was on the other side.

Offers seminars around the country on how to be free from the chains of the past and to live free in Christ.

ᶜᵘ Wounded Heart Ministries, Dan Allender. Offers workshops around the country as well as a newsletter. Call (206) 855-8460 and ask for information.

Counseling

ᶜᵘ Call the Rape Abuse Incest National Network at (800) 656-HOPE. You can speak to an advocate who will help you find resources in your area.

ᶜᵘ Call (719) 531-3400 or write Focus on the Family, Colorado Springs, CO 80995-7451. Limited telephone counseling available. Also the correspondence department can suggest helpful resources.

ᶜᵘ Meier New Life Clinics offer counseling and group therapy. Call (800) 545-1819 and ask for the clinic nearest you.

ᶜᵘ Contact a local pastor and ask for therapists trained in biblical counseling for sexual abuse victims.

Saving the Gift

Come precious daughter,
     You who have set your heart to follow
          after Me, come.
        Raise your eyes. Lift them
           high. . .higher.
Do you see above you the bride draped in
         white? She is lovely in face and form.
         Her smile is radiant, her eyes
         expectant. She is resplendent in beauty,
         bathed in the light of My glory.
         Dignity and character are her
         composure. Purity flows in her wake
         like a bridal train. In her I see no flaw.
    Does she not take your breath away?
    Who is the one I so highly esteem?
    She is you.
Do not shake your head in disbelief, saying,
       "No, Lord, I could never be her."
She is the bride you will become.
Trust Me. I will show you the way to her.
I will guide you and lead you. . .
         one step at a time.

Chapter 12

Capturing the Vision

From:	MFarmington@aol.com
Date:	Friday, January 31, 2003 7:58 AM
To:	Tfarmington@aol.com
Subject:	Help wanted!

Hey, Sis, can't believe your big day is only three months away. I love my brides-maid dress—it's so sleek, not like that horrid green, poofy thing I wore for Betsy's wedding. I chucked that one in the Goodwill box, but I'm not sure even they wanted it.

I'm glad we had a chance to talk over lunch. Thanks for being so real with me and for not judging me. Telling you about what happened between Trevor and me was really hard, especially because you're five years older than I am and you're still a virgin. How do you do it? I mean, you and Chad are SO in love!! I really want to know your secret, especially now that I am committed to making some changes in my life.

Tiff, I meant it when I said that I want to be like you. I did what you said, and God and I had a heart to heart. I know He's forgiven me, and I'm ready to make a fresh start of it. But where do I begin?

Madison

From:	Tfarmington@aol.com
Date:	Friday, January 31, 2003 1:00 PM
To:	Mfarmington@aol.com
Subject:	Coffee Tomorrow

Maddie, your e-mail meant so much to me. Have I told you lately how much I love you? (Oh yeah, yesterday.) But I really do love you, especially your heart and your desire to follow God.

You asked me, "Where do I begin to start over again?" As your big sis, I don't always have all the answers (even though I sometimes act like I do), so it's exciting when I can share something with you that I KNOW will help you!

Do you remember my cute little youth leader in college, the one with the frizzy red hair? She told me something that absolutely changed my life when it came to dealing with guys and the issue of sex. I can't believe I've never shared it with you because this is BIG! She had me do something that saved me from so many bad choices, so many regrets. But I don't want to do this in an e-mail. Tell you what. Why don't you meet me tomorrow after work at that coffee shop across the street from the gym where they serve those great skinny lattes. I'll explain then. See you at 6 p.m.?

Love ya, Maddie,

Tiff

WHAT CHANGED TIFFANY'S LIFE?

We are about to tell you Tiffany's secret. If you wholeheartedly participate in the exercise we are about to recommend, it will impact how you relate to the opposite sex, simplify your dating life, fortify your character, and shape your destiny.

This life-changing exercise involves writing a vision statement that articulates who you want to be on your wedding day. This statement will help you define your dating relationships by identifying who you should spend time with and what to do during that time. But before you can write your vision statement, you must first create a mental picture of yourself on your wedding day.

Did you realize that all things are created twice?[1] All things are created first in the mind and then in actuality. This may sound strange, but think about it. If you want to write a research paper, you first create the report in your mind. You think about what topics you'll cover, which resources you'll need, how you'll begin—all before you actually start to write your paper. If you want to redecorate your apartment, you begin with a mental picture of what you want it to look like. To do this, you ask yourself: What mood do I want to express? What furniture will work? Which colors are best? What accessories? Before your new home can become a physical reality, it must first be a mental creation.

Likewise, if you want to write a vision statement that describes who you want to be on your wedding day, you must first create a mental picture of yourself as that bride.

The following exercise will help you do this. Open your heart and mind to possibilities you may not have considered before. Let your imagination go. Have fun! There is no right or wrong answer. This is simply a time to explore and formulate some of your goals and dreams for the future.

VISUALIZE YOUR WEDDING DAY

Okay, let's begin. Step into the future—today is your wedding day.

Picture your dress, your veil. What do they look like? Are you swathed in lace and pearls or draped in simple elegance? Your hair—is it swept up in a dramatic twist or casually styled?

Visualize your attendants. Who are they? What are they wearing? The expression on their faces—do you see joy?

Is the setting a country church or a regal sanctuary with stained-glass windows? Picture the candles, the flowers. What special touches have your unique signature on them?

Walk down the aisle and visualize the faces in the crowd. Are your neighbors present? Are your classmates or coworkers there? Is your mother in the front row next to Grandma, dabbing her eyes with a hanky? Imagine the thrill of having all the people you love most gathered in one place. People from the past and friends in the present have all joined together to witness this moment that will begin your future.

Now lift your eyes and gaze upon your groom. Does he seem nervous? Is he grinning like a Cheshire cat? What emotions course through you as you join him at his side?

Listen to the words you speak to one another as you pledge your love. Are your vows traditional or did you write them yourselves? Are you gazing deeply into your groom's eyes as you say them? Are you smiling? Crying? So excited you can't contain yourself? Feel the elation as he takes your hand and slips the ring on your finger. Listen to the other words— the words he whispers with his heart that only you can hear...

A voice proclaims, "I now pronounce you man and wife."

It's official—you are married. Suddenly your new husband whisks you away to the reception, and well-wishers mob you both, giving you bear hugs and toasting your future. Camera flashes blind your eyes. You can't hear yourself talk above the din and laughter of the crowd. You dance and smile until your face hurts, all the while counting the minutes until you can be alone with your husband.

Finally the music stops, and your groom carries you away to a place where you can be alone. Chaos is replaced by calm. The public declaration hours earlier was one kind of jubilation; this private declaration will be another. Your husband stands before you, eager to become one with you in every sense of the word. He caresses your face in his hands and searches your eyes. What does he see when he looks at you?

In this critical moment, the moment you have waited for forever, who are you? Are you a woman of conviction, integrity, and moral courage? Do inner strength and holiness characterize your life? Are you clothed in dignity? Does your beloved look at you with wonder and fascination because you cared enough to make a commitment to purity?

Of course, by now you realize that the purpose of this exercise is NOT to crystallize your future wedding plans but to contemplate your character—who you are—on the day of your wedding. We asked you to look at the outward trappings of the ceremony so that you could begin to focus on the inward qualities of your heart. Who you are in this defining moment matters. It matters to you, it matters to your beloved, and it matters to God.

WRITING YOUR VISION STATEMENT

Now that you have a mental image of who you want to be on your wedding day, it's time to put it into words by writing your personal vision statement.

Using four or five sentences, describe who you want to be
when you offer yourself as a Gift to your husband.

Your statement should be as individual as you are. It can take any form: a poem, a prayer, a list, a song, an acrostic, or a simple paragraph. But we warn you, constructing this vision statement won't be easy! Trying to capture an illusive picture with concrete words can be taxing, but it will be worth the effort because this statement will shape the choices you make in the future.

When I (Lorraine) was in charge of media relations for a Fortune 200 company, I had to come up with a one-paragraph vision statement that summarized the purpose of all the activities for my department. It took me months to write that one paragraph, but once my words captured the vision in my head, that vision statement became a guide that clarified which opportunities I should pursue and which to turn down.

Writing your personal vision statement signals to God that you want to be proactive rather than reactive when it comes to sexual purity. Many young women spend more time planning their summer vacations than they do planning their futures, yet it's possible to have a clear picture of who God desires you to be and a specific plan for becoming that woman.

If you are struggling to form the sentences, try making a list of adjectives that you want to describe you as you stand before your new husband. Like a fine-tipped brush, these adjectives will help to paint the detail on the canvas of your vision. Here are a few you might want to consider:

- pure
- morally courageous
- passionate
- honest
- self-controlled
- innocent

- trustworthy
- respectful
- desirable
- faithful
- dignified
- a woman of integrity

We do not know if the young bride in the Song of Solomon made a similar list of attributes, but it's likely that she had given considerable thought about who she wanted to be on her wedding day. As a country maiden about to marry the wealthiest and wisest man in the world, her situation was precarious. Solomon brought palaces, position, and power to their union, but what did she bring? Her gifts were more highly prized than wealth. She was rich in character and rich in purity. We see her new husband reveling in the fact that she has kept the Gift of her body for him alone. "You are like a private garden, my treasure, my bride! You are like a spring that no one else can drink from, a fountain of my own" (Song of Solomon 4:12, NLT). Overwhelmed by the purity and character of his bride, Solomon called his wedding day "the day of his gladness of heart" (3:11).

Following are vision statements from four women. Notice how each reflects the individuality of the writer.

K. J., who is twenty-six and engaged, wrote her vision statement in the form of a prayer that she keeps in her Bible:

Lord, the holiness I desire to have is one You dress me in, one You place upon my being. I want to stand before my future husband in complete purity, not because I have done anything right or noble, but because Your Spirit has called me to holiness, and what You have called me to, You will complete. Present me well, Lord, that on that future day my beloved will feel proud that I honored him by choosing holiness and not selfishness. Continue to implant deep within me a longing for purity, not only in the physical sense, but purity in mind, heart, word, and action. Thank You that You will continue to expand my understanding of what this choice means and what will unfold on that future day.

Jan, forty-seven and formerly married, expressed her vision statement through seven "I will" statements that she made into a bookmark.

Lord, I choose to joyfully partner with You for the rest of my life whether I am single or married. When I realize that I need the touch, companionship, friendship, communication, adoration, or affection of a man,

- I WILL look to You to meet that need. You are my bridegroom and my husband, and no human is as perfect for me as You.
- I WILL strive to have a passion for purity in my dating life.
- I WILL keep my mind and eyes on You and Your perspectives and not succumb to the views of the world.
- I WILL set my mind and heart on You, Lord, through reading Your word, prayer, and worship.
- I WILL, by the power of Your love, be all I can be for You.
- I WILL tell the world about You, my maker and my husband.
- I WILL trust You to show me Your plan for my life and Your provisions for my future.

May people see You reflected in me, and may You receive the glory and honor. I love You.

Jodie, twenty-one, formed her vision statement using a simple acrostic that she cross-stitched and put into a frame on her nightstand:

God,
I ask of Thee
For strength and protection
That I might one day present the Gift wrapped in holiness,
          bound by a ribbon of purity.

Stacey, eighteen, wrote a poem in calligraphy that she matted and framed:

Thank You, Lord, for taking my sin
And making me new.
It is my desire to please You, Lord
In all that I say and do.
Into Your hand I yield my life,
My past, and what is to come.
When I stand one day before my groom,
May You say, "My daughter, 'Well done.'"

We cannot overemphasize the influence your vision statement can have as a guiding force in your life. Keep it in a place where you can review it often. If God's purpose for you includes marriage, and if you focus upon your vision statement and make choices that align with it, the mental image you create will one day be a physical reality.

We encourage you not to move on to the next chapter until your vision statement is complete and you are satisfied that what you've written accurately reflects the desires of your heart. Once you have finished, you will likely feel a sense of accomplishment, and your next thought will be *Okay, now that I have my vision statement, I know* where *I want to go, but* how *do I get there?* In the following chapter you will see a detailed picture of one woman's vision statement and the steps she climbed in order to achieve her goal. The four steps she identified are the same ones that will help you to move forward in your commitment.

Chapter 13

A Step in the Right Direction

Imagine that you are standing at the bottom of a flight of stairs. Now look up. At the top of the stairs, see the image you created through your vision statement. This is your goal. How do you reach it? You could bend your knees, thrust your arms upward, and try to leap to the top in a single bound, but that might result in a few broken bones. No, the best way to reach your goal—the surest and safest way to get to the top—is one step at a time.

The climb can actually be a joy UNLESS you get distracted and lose sight of your goal. If this happens you may find yourself headed in a direction you never intended.

Lorraine: A voice crackled over the loudspeaker: "Final boarding call for Flight 1407." Linda and I were en route to Alaska to teach at an Intimate Issues conference. We walked up to the gate and looked out the window at our plane. Because of the distance of the flight, we had expected to fly on a roomy 747, but the plane in front of us looked more like a child's toy. To make matters worse, instead of boarding through a nice dry Jetway as we normally did for our flights, the attendant told us we would have to walk a hundred yards to the plane—in the pouring rain.

Linda grimaced as she looked down at the expensive ivory crocheted shoes she'd just purchased. "My wonderful shoes," she wailed. "I can't ruin my new shoes!" Ducking her head, she pulled up the hood of her burgundy raincoat and raced across the tarmac with only one thought on her mind: getting her new shoes out of the rain.

Momentarily delayed by a baggage attendant who wanted to check my laptop computer, I was surprised by what I saw when I looked up. To my left, a line of passengers marched single file up the flight of stairs that led into the small airplane. To my right, a burgundy raincoat marched up another flight of stairs—stairs that led nowhere! In her obsession to get her shoes out of the rain, Linda had begun climbing the stairs that had been pulled away from the loading dock in order to make room for the plane. The only thing at the top of those stairs was air!

"Linda!" I called.

But the burgundy coat climbed upward.

"Linda!" I shouted again, trying not to laugh. The people behind me chuckled softly as they watched my friend march up the steps with focused determination.

"Linda!" I hollered at the top of my lungs.

She looked up and then turned around. The startled look on her face when she realized where she was caused me—and everyone else on the tarmac—to double over with laughter.

She marched back down the stairs, head down, studying her very wet shoes. When she came near enough to hear, I smiled sweetly, "Want to join the rest of us on the airplane?"

"Don't you ever breathe a word of this to anybody," she mumbled.

"I won't," I promised, but my fingers were crossed.

As you probably guessed, there is a point to this story—never buy expensive shoes and then walk in the rain! Actually, this story wonderfully illustrates the importance of seeing your goal before you begin to climb. As the saying goes, if you aim at nothing, you will hit it every time. But if you aim toward a picture that you have thoughtfully created, prayed over, and are committed to, you will get there…one step at a time.

We want to introduce you to a very special woman, our friend Nancy Barton. Nancy has learned to move forward, one step at a time, in her vision statement.

NANCY'S VISION

Nancy has spent many years in the trenches of singleness. As the women's ministry director at a large church, she ministers to women who are predominately married with children, or, as she says, "Women who have what I want." Nancy knew that if she were to thrive in this culture (and not merely survive), she had to have a plan, a proactive strategy that would help her manage the many challenges of being single in a couple's world.

Nancy's vision statement is short and concise. Expressed through four "I choose" statements, her vision is an outward expression of her inward desire to please God and follow Him. Here is what she wrote:

> *I choose to partner with Jesus.* I will live every day acknowledging my Savior in all I say and do.

> *I choose to give my affections to God.* I will devote myself to the Lord and seek His wisdom in maneuvering the many moral decisions I must make.

> *I choose to set my heart and mind on Christ.* I will focus on the things of Christ, not on the things of this earth.

> *I choose to live up to my full potential.* I will strive for abundant living in my singleness.

We found Nancy's vision statement inspiring, but reading it raised questions. What does "partnering with Jesus" look like? Practically speaking, how do you give your affections to God? What steps do you take in order to set your heart and mind on Christ? Are there certain things you can do, attitudes you can adopt that make it easier for you to live to your full potential?

We asked Nancy to explain each of her four "I choose" statements and to describe some of the steps she took (and is still taking) to live out her vision. Here is what she wrote:

Partnering with Jesus

I remember vividly when I first understood what it meant to partner with Jesus. It was a few days before my company's annual Christmas party. It came to my attention that I might be one of the few singles in attendance. It was such a dreadful thought, and of course, I truly didn't want to go! But as I prayed, I realized that God wanted me to go, and HE wanted to be my partner. I didn't know how this could happen, but I began to pray that I would recognize His presence beside me every moment and that I would radiate that presence. So "we" went to the party!

As "we" entered, I immediately saw a potential male interest with a beautiful woman. It didn't phase me. As "we" walked from room to room, I socialized, encouraged those I saw, and truly practiced putting others first. As "we" left that evening and got into my car for the long drive home, I burst into tears…tears of joy and pain. I rejoiced to feel the peace and presence of Jesus in a tangible way, despite the pain of singleness.

The following Monday a friend stopped by my office and said, "I noticed you at the party and wondered if it might be hard for you to be there alone. But I just wanted to tell you that you radiated God's joy that night."

Since then, I've attended countless weddings, receptions, class reunions, and parties with Jesus as my partner. I can't say it's been easy, but I know that with each event my faith has grown. Jesus is a real, tangible presence—as real to me as any other person. I continue to grow in my understanding of what it means to partner with Him daily in the small things and the big things and what it means for Him to be the ever-present, always available lover of my soul.

Giving my affections to God

If I'd known when I was twenty-five that I would still be single at age forty-four, I would have said to the Lord, "Stop this planet, I want off." Sharing my life with someone spiritually, emotionally, and physically is all I've ever really wanted. The idea of living life without a sexual relationship appalls me and, at times, seems so unfair. But as I practice giving God my affections, I recognize that He will give me the power and ability to live my life with purity in my words, thoughts, and actions. And to feel contentment. He will never give me more than I can bear—that's His promise.

I've often felt like my sexual desires are as strong as a man's. Still, I believe that God knows this and is giving me the power to live uprightly. I have asked the Lord to guide me in my thoughts and actions and to keep all evil far from me. Whether it's a movie, date, visual or mental image, magazine, or song, I've learned to run from temptation. By that, I mean that I literally turn my body or mind the opposite way.

I've also asked God to keep me from dating out of subtle reasons of loneliness, insecurities, and fears. I've asked Him to circumvent men who may be interested in me but not be the best for me so as to prevent any unnecessary investments of time and affections on something destined for failure. These are hard prayers to pray, but ultimately I know it is for my good. Still, there are days I literally cry out to Him with my longing to be married. Yet I'm so thankful for the privilege He's given me to find Him to be my bridegroom now.

Setting my heart and mind on Christ
I know that the barometer of my single state is measured greatly by whether I choose to set my heart and mind on things above or on the things of this world. It takes a constant turning of my thoughts away from envy, comparison, and jealousy of those around me to turn my face to Jesus. Since I've been raised to a new life, I am to live that new life with Christ.

Sadly, I can get so consumed by my longings that I miss the

incredible joy and excitement of this present life with my Lord. I deeply regret the days I've spent complaining, pining, and sulking...all because I focused on this earthly life! As I memorize Scripture and worship, I ask God to lift my eyes to His heavenly purposes. Keeping verses before me as I exercise, relax, stop at a light, or wait in the doctor's office helps me maintain this perspective. I not only memorize the verse but offer it to the Lord as a prayer.

In recent years, I've enjoyed growing as a worshiper. I've cried through countless worship experiences, both at home and in church, as I realize that Jesus loves me more completely than any man ever could. Because I love dancing, I often picture myself swaying back and forth, dancing with Jesus. Those moments are pure bliss as I am engulfed in His love for me and hear Him say, "Nancy, you are my beautiful bride."

Living up to my full potential

I sometimes ask myself if I'm really living to my full potential. Am I truly being all my Lord would have me to be? I grieve over the countless days I've wasted, longing for what I didn't have. I no longer put life on hold. Instead I pray, *God, take me, mold me, fill me, and use me NOW.* I realize that the conforming and molding He is doing in my life to prepare me to be His bride is also being used to prepare me to become the bride of my future husband.

I can't believe Jesus is satisfied with my using only 50 or 60 percent of my potential. He wants 100 percent! I refuse to allow my singleness to handicap me in my ability to live a fully committed life to God. I desire to learn how to live in the abundance of Christ in such a way that my life will be a message of inner strength and holiness. I anticipate the day when I will exchange gifts with my husband; may he find a woman clothed with strength and dignity, wrapped up in love, and opened only for her beloved.

As Nancy has walked through the days of her singleness, she has lived the following verses:

Look straight ahead, and fix your eyes on what lies before you.
Mark out a straight path for your feet; then stick to the path and
stay safe. (Proverbs 4:25-26, NLT)

We pray you, too, will fix your eyes on what lies before you. May focusing on your vision statement create a straight path upon which your feet can walk. As we talked with Nancy and other single women about what encourages them to make their vision statement a reality, we discovered four choices that propelled them toward their goal. These same four steps will help you move forward in your vision statement.

Step One: Set Your heart

Step Two: Renew Your Mind

Step Three: Control Your Body

Step Four: Strengthen Your Will

Come with us on a walk, and let's climb each step together.

Chapter 14

Set Your Heart

What does your heart desire? When we ask women this question, the answers vary. But if they are single, almost without exception one of their answers is "I want to get married someday."

Does your future include a husband? Only God knows the answer to that question, but we do know that He delights in bringing a man and a woman together in marriage. God is the Divine Matchmaker. He brought Eve to Adam (Genesis 2:22). He brought Rebekah to Isaac (Genesis 24:7). He brought Rachel to Jacob (Genesis 29:9-11). If marriage is part of His plan for you, He will bring you together with your husband. Trust God in this. Believe that He truly has your best interest at heart and that He will bring the right man at the right time.

SET YOUR HEART ON GOD

Lorraine: From the moment I met "Eric," I felt certain he was the one for me. His dazzling smile and infectious laugh instantly captured my heart, but it was his voice, his rich full voice, that made my knees weak. A born romantic, Eric appeared one night below my bedroom window with his guitar to serenade me. I loved it—so did the sixty other girls in my sorority.

We talked into the wee hours of the morning, discovering everything we could about one another. We couldn't bear to be apart. We studied together and held hands at concerts and football games. Eric was everything to me, and when he took me home to meet his family, it was easy for me to see myself being a part of their lives.

The weekend he came to meet my mom and stepdad we had planned to express to them our desire to be married. But Eric acted strangely. We had a fight, and the subject was not brought up. On the six-hour drive back to the university, Eric told me that he had changed his mind. He didn't want to marry me. In fact, he wanted to date other people. He didn't love me: He felt I was really more of a sister to him. I thought, *Who are you kidding? You'd be put in jail if you kissed your sister the way you've kissed me.*

A myriad of emotions assaulted me: anger, hurt, betrayal, denial, disbelief. I stared out the window and watched the blur of the landscape pass by. *Why God? Why is this happening?*

Over the next few days I physically experienced withdrawal symptoms from Eric: nausea, vomiting, sleeplessness, dizziness, and the sweats. My eyes were bloodshot from crying. People talked to me, but I couldn't hear what they were saying. After a week the shock wore off and anger set in. I was mad at Eric. Mad at the world. Mad at God. In my mind I screamed at God.

> *God, You are so cruel! You have taken*
> *away from me every man I have ever loved—*
> *my dad, my high school boyfriend, and now Eric.*
> *Why do You hate me so?*
> *If this is the kind of God You are,*
> *I never want anything to do with You ever again.*

But even as I shouted the words, I knew they weren't true. I couldn't live without God. I needed Him. As angry and hurt as I was, I couldn't walk away from Him.

Six months later I had cooled down and learned to accept life without Eric. One morning I opened my Bible and read through several psalms. I felt closer to God than I had in quite some time. Again I asked, *Why did this happen, God? Did I love Eric too much?* I hadn't really expected an answer, but God spoke clearly to my heart. *No, Lorraine. You didn't love Eric too much. You loved Me too little.*

It was true! Instead of focusing on God, all of my time, energy, devotion, and love had been poured into Eric. I was appalled when I realized what I had done. I had made Eric my god.

"I'm sorry, God," I cried. "Please forgive me. I promise never again to make another person my god."

I wrote this in my Bible: "I will make no other person or thing my god. I will put no other person or thing in charge of my joy."

Many times I have thanked the Lord for circumventing my will and establishing His will in my life. Almost twenty-five years ago I married Peter Pintus, and it is impossible for me to imagine being married to anyone else. Peter is God's best for me. When we were engaged, I told Peter that I loved him but that he could never rate higher than "second" with me because God was first. He said that was okay because I'd never get higher than second with him either!

Friend, this is critical:

Set your heart on God, not on another person.

When we talk about your heart, we are using the word to mean the very center and core of your life. In the biblical sense the heart is not seen as the body's blood pump but as the center and focus of one's inner personal life: the source of motivation, the seat of passion, the spring of all thought processes, particularly the conscience.[1]

Make God your passion. Devote yourself to Him. Make Him your first love. See to it that all other pursuits and devotions take a dim second to Him and that He is high and exulted in your life. Say with the psalmist:

My heart is steadfast, O God, my heart is steadfast.
(Psalm 108:1, NRSV)

Take your heart rate: Is your heart set on God?

SET YOUR HEART ON PURITY

Blessed are the pure in heart, for they shall see God. (Matthew 5:8)

To "see God" means to enjoy Him personally, to perceive who He is and know His ways and His character. Do you want to see God? Be pure in heart! "The pure in heart are the single-minded who are free from the tyranny of a divided self, and do not try to serve God and the world at the same time."[2] The cry of our hearts must be "God, give me an undivided heart!" This single-minded focus on the Lord Jesus will stir within us a desire to keep ourselves pure, just as Christ is pure (1 John 3:3).

Purity is freedom from anything improper...from anything that defiles or contaminates.[3] The word *pure* means "unmixed with any other substance."

One single woman observed: "The only teaching most singles have heard on purity is 'just don't do it.' There's too much focus on 'going all the way' and not on the greater issue of purity. Purity is more than not doing certain things; it's an attitude. If we are asking the question, 'How far can I go?' that's the wrong question."

We agree! And we add, *purity is a* lifelong *attitude and approach to a relationship.*

We were teaching a Bible study to a group of thirty single women. When we made the statement that purity is also important in marriage, they looked surprised. Their goal was to "stay pure until the wedding night." The unspoken thought was *After the wedding night I will no longer have to fight this battle of sexual purity.*

Wrong. Purity is a daily choice—before and after marriage. Before marriage, purity is faithfulness to God to remain sexually pure. After marriage, purity is faithfulness to God to pursue sexual joy and fulfillment with only one's husband.

Marriage should be honored by all, and the marriage bed kept pure.
(Hebrews 13:4, NIV)

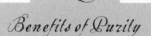

Benefits of Purity

Praise the LORD, O my soul, and forget not all his benefits. (Psalm 103:2, NIV)

Oh, the blessings and benefits of following God's plan! He says wait because He loves you and wants to protect you. Remind yourself continually that as you commit to sexual purity, you will be

> Free from regret, guilt, or shame
> Free from the fear of pregnancy
> Free from the adoption decision
> Free from the physical and emotional problems associated with abortion
> Free from sexually transmitted diseases
> Free from marrying too soon
> Free from the guilt of knowing you were part of another person's sin
> Free from the pain of disappointing those who trust and love you

You will not only be free FROM negative consequences but free TO enjoy the positive.

> Free to pursue life goals
> Free to respect yourself and others
> Free to establish trust in marriage
> Free to anticipate the joy of your wedding night
> Free to enjoy and discover your husband's body without comparison

This verse teaches that both single and married women should honor marriage and that both single and married women should keep the marriage bed pure. We could paraphrase Hebrews 13:4 like this: "Set your hopes and dreams on marriage. And into that marriage bed allow only one person—your husband. Don't adulterate that relationship with anyone else—not even ghosts from your past."

Take your heart rate: Is your heart set on purity?

SET YOUR HEART ON LOVING

Beloved, if God so loved us, we also ought to love one another.
(1 John 4:11)

The Greek language has four different words for the word *love*. One word is *eros*, which is the term used for sexual love. Our Lord encourages deep exploration of the passion of *eros* love—in marriage. Another word is *agape*. This kind of love can be practiced whether you are married or single. *Agape* is a selfless, unconditional love. It is the kind of giving, sacrificial love God expresses toward you, the kind of love that caused Jesus to die for you. The basis of this love is summarized in Philippians 2:3 (NIV):

Do nothing out of selfish ambition or vain conceit, but in humility consider others as better than yourselves.

Immediately following this verse, Paul adds: "Your attitude should be the same as that of Christ Jesus" (verse 5, NIV). Christ's love for us is *agape;* He wants to develop *agape* love in us so that we may express it to others—and this includes boyfriends and fiancés. Learning to love with the sacrificial love of Christ is a lifelong process. First Corinthians 13 practically shows what this *agape* love looks like:

Love is patient and kind. Love is not jealous or boastful or proud or rude. Love does not demand its own way. Love is not irritable, and it keeps no record of when it has been wronged. It is never glad about injustice but rejoices whenever the truth wins out. Love never gives up, never loses faith, is always hopeful, and endures through every circumstance.

Love will last forever. (1 Corinthians 13:4-8, NLT)

Linda: I was a new bride when a friend suggested I take this beautiful passage and put my name in place of the word *love*. She told me, "Say it out loud, and look in the mirror while you say it." So I started out. "Linda is patient and kind" (gulp). "Linda is not jealous or boastful or proud or rude" (double gulp). "Linda does not demand her own way." (There weren't enough gulps.) I couldn't go on. The words just didn't sound right—they were too far from the truth. But this unpleasant exercise motivated me to begin to pray that God would teach me to "*agape* love" this new husband of mine.

During your single years, God wants you to concentrate on building nonsexual *agape* love rather than *eros* love. So let's get practical; take the love passage, and think of ways you can reach out to the special one in your life with *agape* love.

Love is patient. "I can intently listen to him talk about football when it means nothing to me."

Love is kind. "I can type his term paper for him."

Love is not jealous. "I can encourage him to spend time with 'the guys.'"

Love is not rude. "I can talk to him with the same tone I use with my pastor."

Love does not demand it's own way. "I can seek to discover where he wants to go to dinner, which movie he wants to see."

Love is not irritable. "I can be pleasant when he promises to call and then doesn't."

Love never gives up. "I can persist in prayer for him."

Love is always hopeful. "I can focus on the ways I've seen him grow when his shortcomings present themselves."

Will you take a step and learn to love in nonsexual ways by developing *agape* love? Now, before you are a bride, is the time to practice. Tuck 1 Corinthians 13 away in your mind and heart, meditate on it, and pray it back to God. Ask Him how you can practically apply it now. One young woman's honest prayer sounded like this:

> *God, I've got a long way to go… I've thought of love in terms*
> *of what a man will give to me. Teach me how to*
> *love with a giving,* agape *love. I'm not very patient or very kind…*
> *sometimes I'm rude, and I definitely want my own way.*
> *And, oh, God, I do get irritable,*
> *and I keep a whole list of his wrongs.*
> *Work in me, God. I need to grow.*
> *I don't think I know what love really is all about.*
> *But I want to know.*
> *Teach me to have this "never give up, never lose faith" love.*

Take your heart rate: Is your heart set on *agape* loving?

SET YOUR HEART ON PRAYER

The earnest prayer of a righteous person has great power and wonderful results. (James 5:16, NLT)

You don't know whether your future husband is a tall, dark athlete or a blond, blue-eyed genius. You don't know if he was born on a farm in Nebraska or to a wealthy family in Japan. Some authors encourage young women to make a wish list of things they want in their future husband, everything from his shoe size to his craving for feta cheese. While such an exercise can be helpful because it makes your future spouse seem more real, we discourage detailed shopping lists focused on personality traits and physical attributes.

Instead of making a shopping list, we recommend that you pray specifically and frequently for your future mate's spiritual growth. Even though you may not yet know the man you will marry, praying for him allows you to participate now in who he will become. And God says that your prayer has great power and wonderful results. What an exciting promise!

One college girl wrote:

> I pray for my future husband every night, even though I have no idea who he is. I pray that he will grow strong in the Lord, strive to do His will, have a strong desire to obey Him in every situation, and that he will always love the Lord more than he loves me. The more I pray for him, the more special he becomes. The more special he becomes, the more I want to save myself for him.[4]

You can pray for your future husband, but you can also pray for the one you are dating. Prayer is a way of saying, "I love you." Prayer for another is a gift given in secret that delights the heart of God and changes the one you lift in prayer. The deeper you grow in knowing someone, the more you see his strengths and weaknesses. In prayer you can thank God for the strengths and ask Him to build up the weak areas. Who cares enough to pray consistently for the man in your life? Maybe only you.

Here are some suggestions for what you can pray:

- Read a chapter of Proverbs every day, and pray the wisdom principles for him.
- Read Galatians 5:22-23, and pray for God to develop a fruit of the spirit in his life. For example, on Monday pray for God to teach him how to love. On Tuesday, pray for joy to characterize his life. Continue on through the other fruits of peace, patience, kindness, goodness, faithfulness, gentleness, and self-control.
- Pray 1 Corinthians 13:4-8 for him, asking God to make him a man who loves with *agape* love.

Take your heart rate: Is your heart set on prayer?

The following beautiful hymn by Charles Wesley expresses the joy of setting your heart on God, on purity, on loving, and on prayer.

O, for a heart to praise my God
A heart from sin set free
A heart that always feels Thy blood
So freely shed for me.
A heart resigned, submissive, meek
My Great Redeemer's Throne
Where only Christ is heard to speak
Where Jesus reigns alone.
A heart in every thought renewed
And full of love divine
Perfect and right, pure and good:
A copy, Lord, of Thine.

You have your vision statement before you. You've taken the first step by setting your heart. Now let's take the second step: Renew your mind.

Chapter 15

Renew Your Mind

Unless you are a nun cloistered away behind high walls or a cave dweller in the middle of the Gobi Desert, sexual images from the media continually assault you.

Not a day goes by—NOT A SINGLE DAY—in which you are not forced to deal with a wrong message about sex. Hollywood infuses sexual suggestions into every television show and movie, right down to children's cartoons. Ads selling everything from toothpaste to paper towels carry sexual innuendos. Billboards blare at you, newspaper headlines scream at you. You can't even buy a pack of mints at the grocery store without inadvertently learning from the tabloids about the latest sexual escapades of politicians or celebrities.

If you think this sexual saturation doesn't affect you, think again. All the messages you have ever heard and seen about sex, those you willingly exposed yourself to and those that were thrust upon you, have come together to form in you a sexual mind-set. A mind-set is a collection of individual thoughts that, over a period of time, influence the way we perceive life.[1]

Your sexual mind-set is unique, unlike that of anyone else. No one else has your exact set of information and experiences. Everything you have seen related to sex, everything you have heard, every right sexual choice you've made, every wrong choice, any harm that may have been done to you sexually—all have contributed to the mind-set you have today.

What is your sexual mind-set? If you are like most women, you may not know because you've never considered the cumulative effect of your experiences and their impact upon your thinking. At our Intimate Issues conferences, we ask women to participate in an exercise that helps them get a picture of their sexual mind-set. We are going to ask you to do this exercise as well because an accurate picture of your mind-set is vital to your ability to pursue sexual purity.

FLOWERS OR WEEDS?

Take a moment and quiet yourself—clear all thoughts from your mind. Once your mind is clear, picture a flower bed with nothing growing in it.[2] This flower bed represents your sexual mind-set when you were born. As a baby, you had no impressions about sex—your mind only had bare soil. But as you grew, seeds were scattered on the flower bed of your mind. These seeds produced either flowers (uplifting thoughts about the beauty and holiness of sex that conformed to God's purpose for the Gift) or weeds (ugly, deceiving, or shameful thoughts that perverted God's purpose for sex).

Now try to remember the first thing you ever heard about sex. How old were you? Who told you? What was said? What seed was planted, a weed or a flower?

Think back to the next message you heard. Maybe it was a picture you saw or something you learned from your friends or siblings. Try to recall when you studied the reproductive system in elementary school. How did the teacher explain intercourse? What were your thoughts? Did your classmates snicker or make snide comments? What seeds were planted, weeds or flowers?

What did you learn about sex from your parents? Your grandparents? What conversations did you have with friends or classmates?

As you got older, what seeds did the images and messages you saw on television, movies, or in magazines sow? What sexual situations did you unintentionally witness? What did you purposefully expose yourself to? Were there any situations where something was forced upon you?

Each of these seeds ultimately produced a weed or a flower. Visualize each one growing in the soil of your mind. Take your time. Don't skip anything. Before you can transform your mind you must first have an accurate picture of what has been planted there.

After you've considered every thought or image you can remember, stand back and survey the scene. What do you see? A lovely garden with splashes of color and inviting fragrances (with a large section reserved for planting roses with your future husband) or an ugly, untended place, full of weeds and in need of some serious attention?

Most of us do not grow up with God's perspective of sex, so we need to ask Him to transform our mind-set. Paul writes about how to do this in the book of Romans.

> Do not be conformed to this world, but be transformed by the renewing of your mind, that you may prove what is that good and acceptable and perfect will of God. (Romans 12:2, NKJV)

Our sexual mind-sets are transformed through two actions. First, we must resolve not to conform to the world. Second, we must renew our minds.

DO NOT CONFORM: PULL WEEDS

Do not be conformed to this world. (Romans 12:2, NKJV)

When you visualized the flower bed of your mind, you saw where your attitudes about sex originated. Let's focus for a moment on the weeds. Some of the weeds you pictured cropped up only recently. Others have been there for a long time and have developed an extensive root system.

There is no weed that God cannot pull out. We have seen Him pull out, in an instant, weeds that seemed as large as trees. He can do that! Other times, He removes them through a process. But always, always God will remove the weeds if we are faithful to allow Him into our lives. Please don't wait any longer. Invite Him now to begin to remove the weeds, and trust Him as He does the work that is necessary to begin this transformation. You could pray something like this.

> *Lord, I had no idea there was so much junk in my mind.*
> *I want it out. Please reach in and pull out the weeds*
> *of wrong thinking about sex.*
> *And then show me how to change the way I think.*

After weeding the flower bed, it is time to plant some colorful flower seeds deep in the soil.

RENEW YOUR MIND: PLANT FLOWERS

Be transformed by the renewing of your mind. (Romans 12:2, NKJV)

In the original Greek the word translated in Romans 12:2 as *transformed* is the word *metamophoo,* from which we get the word *metamorphosis.*[3] Just as the caterpillar crawling in the dust is motivated to make its way up a tree to spin a cocoon, eventually emerging as a beautiful butterfly, so this command should motivate us to be transformed by the renewing of our minds. So how does your mind become a place of beauty? Let us suggest four things you can do that will result in a flourishing flower garden in your mind.

1. Read the Word. God's Word is living and active, sharper than a two-edged sword. It has the ability to discern everything about you and change you (Hebrews 4:12). You need to know God's perspective about sexuality as presented in His Word. We challenge you to faithfully read the Scriptures and also to read books like this one that expound upon God's perspective of sex. Just think! With every page you have turned while reading this book, you have been planting colorful tulips in the flower bed of your mind.

2. *Study the Word.* We hope that you are already doing the eight-week Bible study at the end of this book. If not, begin now. When you dig in deeply and study God's Word, it allows the seeds you have planted to germinate.

3. *Memorize the Word.* The most effective way we know to transform your mind is to memorize Scripture. God has transformed our sexual mind-sets by planting seeds of Scripture in the soil of our minds. These seeds have blossomed into a fragrant and beautiful multicolored flower bed. And God desires to do the same thing for you! Memorizing Scripture is never easy, but we testify to you that it is well worth the effort.

When you memorize Scripture about God's view of sex, you increase the Holy Spirit's vocabulary in your life and change your sexual mind-set.[4] What is God's viewpoint? The Most High God says the sexual relationship in marriage is holy—so holy that the physical intimacy between a husband and wife is a picture of the spiritual intimacy that God desires with you (Ephesians 5:31-32). A good place to begin planting the flowers of God's perspective would be to memorize these two verses.

> For this reason a man shall leave his father and mother and shall be
> joined to his wife, and the two shall become one flesh. This mystery
> is great; but I am speaking with reference to Christ and the church.

Reading, studying, and memorizing Scripture are critical in the process of transforming your mind, but they require less explanation than the next discipline: meditation. All four are important, but because many women have misconceptions about what meditation is or how a Christian should use it, we will focus on this subject at length.

4. *Meditate on the Word.* According to *Merriam-Webster's Dictionary, meditate* means "to focus one's thoughts upon, to ponder or contemplate." Meditation sends the roots of Scripture down deep as you personalize what you've memorized and pray it back to God. One of the synonyms given in the dictionary for *meditate* is the word *ruminate.*

Bessie the cow has a most unusual way of digesting her food. Early in the morning she strolls among the bluegrass, snatching up as much as she can eat. Then about ten in the morning, when the sun becomes hot, she lies down in the shade and regurgitates the food out of her first stomach chamber, called the rumen. (Yes, we agree, this is rather gross.) This time Bessie chews the grass thoroughly. The food then goes into stomachs two, three, and four. Eventually the digested food is absorbed into her bloodstream and becomes part of her life.[5]

Why are we telling you about the disgusting way cows digest their food? There is a point. *Rumination* and *meditation* are parallel words. Just as Bessie "meditated" on her bluegrass, and it became part of her, when you meditate on God's Word, it becomes a part of you. Each time you bring up God's truth that you have placed in your mind and "chew on it," letting it sink deeply into your heart, it becomes more and more a part of you.

One young woman meditated on Ephesians 5:31-32 and personalized it by praying it back to God:

> *God, I want to get my arms around the idea*
> *that You think sex is holy. I am amazed that You say*
> *sexual intimacy in marriage is a picture of the spiritual intimacy*
> *You want with me. This really blows me away.*
> *Please take this truth and make it real in my mind.*
> *I want to be changed!*

Lorraine: One of the most life-changing verses I have ever memorized and meditated upon is Philippians 4:8:

> Finally, brethren, whatever is true, whatever is honorable, whatever
> is right, whatever is pure, whatever is lovely, whatever is of good
> repute, if there is any excellence and if anything worthy of praise,
> dwell on these things.

For many years my mind-set about sex looked more like a condemned weed lot than a flower garden. When I was single, I didn't understand God's perspective of sex. I made wrong choices and exposed myself to things that were contrary to God's law. Weeds grew rampant—and I let them remain for many years.

When I finally realized how far apart my thinking was from His, I begged the Lord to transform my mind. This transformation began by memorizing Philippians 4:8. Then I meditated upon it, and God and I would have these dialogues. God would point to the weed and ask, "Lorraine, is this weed true?" I'd say, "No, Lord, please pull it out." Then He would point to a different weed and say, "Is this weed honorable? Is it right and pure?" And I'd say, "No, Lord, pull it out." Then God would bring a holy thought about sex that aligned with His Word and ask, "Lorraine, is this thought excellent and worthy of praise?" And my heart would cry, "Yes, Lord!" And He'd say, "Dwell on this."

In this way God transformed my sexual mind-set one weed, one flower at a time. If you could peek into the flower bed in my mind, you would see something that resembles a quaint English garden, complete with a wicker bench—a place where I can sit and enjoy the beauty God has grown there. However, this garden requires daily maintenance. I still use Philippians 4:8 like a garden spade to help me "pull" and "plant."

Memorizing and meditating require commitment. Perhaps you are asking, "Is it worth the effort?" We could tell you many stories of women who would answer that question with a resounding yes, but we'll just tell you about one.

Linda: During a weekend retreat, Gena asked to speak privately with me. Out poured a story of heartache and pain. Six months before, after her husband had left for work and before she left for her office, a man broke in their house and brutally raped her. Tears streamed down her face as she said, "Linda, I can't make love with my husband. The images of what I saw and heard replay like a videotape in my mind. I can't bear it." As we wept together, I prayed over Gena and begged God to clear out the horror in her mind.

When she turned to leave, I was aware that God had worked in her heart but that she would need encouragement in the coming days. I said, "Gena, we've asked God to root out the horrible images. Now you must plant the flower seeds of His Word in their place. Will you memorize and

Flower Seeds

Here are a few flower seeds of Scripture to plant:

Do not stir up nor awaken love until it pleases. (Song of Solomon 2:7, NKJV)

Flee sexual immorality. (1 Corinthians 6:18, NKJV)

But among you there must not be even a hint of sexual immorality, or of any kind of impurity…because these are improper for God's holy people. (Ephesians 5:3, NIV)

Now flee from youthful lusts and pursue righteousness, faith, love and peace, with those who call on the Lord from a pure heart. (2 Timothy 2:22)

Other Scripture you might want to memorize:

But immorality or any impurity or greed must not even be named among you, as is proper among saints; and there must be no filthiness and silly talk, or coarse jesting, which are not fitting, but rather giving of thanks. (Ephesians 5:3-4)

Whatever is true, whatever is honorable, whatever is right, whatever is pure, whatever is lovely, whatever is of good repute, if there is any excellence and if anything worthy of praise, dwell on these things. (Philippians 4:8)

meditate on one verse of Scripture about the beauty of God's Gift of sex every week for the next four weeks?" Gena agreed and promised to e-mail me in four weeks and tell me what God had done.

Four weeks passed and no e-mail. Two more weeks and then her

Let marriage be held in honor by all, and let the marriage bed be kept undefiled. (Hebrews 13:4, NRSV)

All discipline for the moment seems not to be joyful, but sorrowful; yet to those who have been trained by it, afterwards it yields the peaceful fruit of righteousness. (Hebrews 12:11)

Keep watching and praying that you may not enter into temptation; the spirit is willing, but the flesh is weak. (Matthew 26:41)

I have chosen the faithful way. (Psalm 119:30)

I have set the LORD continually before me; because He is at my right hand, I will not be shaken. (Psalm 16:8)

Commit your works to the LORD and your plans will be established. (Proverbs 16:3)

Search me, O God, and know my heart; try me and know my anxious thoughts; and see if there be any hurtful way in me, and lead me in the everlasting way. (Psalm 139:23-24)

And the LORD will continually guide you, and satisfy your desire in scorched places, and give strength to your bones; and you will be like a watered garden, and like a spring of water whose waters do not fail. (Isaiah 58:11)

e-mail arrived in my in-box. This is what she said: "Linda, I did what you asked not for four weeks but for six weeks, and last night, for the first time since the rape, my husband and I made love and there were no flash-backs!"

The Word of God transforms minds! If He can transform Gena's mind, He can also transform yours.

One of the sweetest scents that lingers in a garden planted with God's perspective is the fragrance of purity. Purity delights God. Is there anything we can do to promote purity? That's a good question. The psalmist also asks: "How can a young [woman] keep [her] way pure?" (Psalm 119:9, NIV). And the answer is given: "I have hidden your word in my heart that I might not sin against you" (119:11, NIV).

Did you get that? Did it sink in? God's way to stay pure is to plant His Word in your heart! When you read, study, memorize, and meditate on God's Word, not only does God transform your mind; He also releases the fragrance of purity in your life. This scent is a pleasing aroma—to God, to you, and to your future spouse.

Let's take inventory of where we are. You have written your vision statement; your goal is before you. You have set your heart and seen how to begin renewing your mind. What's next? Get ready. It's time to learn to control your body.

Passages for reading and meditation:

1 Thessalonians 4:3-4	Psalm 37:1-7
Proverbs 2	Psalm 73:25-26
Proverbs 3:5-6	Psalm 19:7-14
Proverbs 4:18-27	Psalm 86:11-13
Psalm 1:1-3	Isaiah 40:28-31

Chapter 16

Control Your Body

We told the women at one of our Intimate Issues conferences that we were going to laugh about the body, and we did laugh—so hard that tears were streaming down many faces. Then we asked a sobering question that silenced the laughter. "How many of you would say you are satisfied with your body?" Eyes searched the room to see if *any* woman was pleased with everything about her body—the shape of her legs, the look of her face, the color of her hair, her shoe size, and her cup size...

In a crowded room of nine hundred women, one brave soul raised her hand.

If Meg Ryan had been in the audience that day, even she would not have raised her hand. Meg, who we think has an enviable body punctuated with an adorable smile, says, "I think I'm kind of weird looking. If I could change the way I look, I'd like to have longer legs, smaller feet, a smaller nose...."[1]

What is wrong with us? Why are we as women often so critical about the way we look?

One reason could be that most of us suffer from a disease called "compare-itis." Women are born comparers. Comparing is not something we do consciously—it is intrinsically woven into our femaleness. We compare prices when we shop. We compare tastes when we eat. And when we walk into a room full of women, we compare our bodies with their bodies.

Get ready for a startling fact. *There are three billion women in the world and only eight supermodels.* Yet for some reason we always end up comparing ourselves to those eight airbrushed beauties. No wonder we feel like we don't measure up!

Merchandisers capitalize on this tendency. Why do you think there are more pictures of women in women's magazines than there are pictures of women in men's magazines? (Pornography is the exception.) They know that we will compare ourselves to the fashion model smiling from the slick paper and find ourselves lacking. Then maybe, just maybe, we will buy their tummy-tucking swimsuit in hopes that it will magically transform us into the beauty on the page! (Fat chance.)

We, too, suffer from this disease. Last week Linda went to the gym. After comparing her body to everyone else in the room, she proudly thought, *I'm the thinnest one here.* But later, when the younger crowd showed up for their workouts, she looked at one buff body and thought, *My right thigh is bigger than her waist.*

All this comparing does not please God. His Word says that when we compare ourselves with others, we are foolish (2 Corinthians 10:12, NLT). Not only are we foolish, but we can also seriously hinder our ability to maintain a healthy sexual mind-set.

Our feelings about our bodies affect our ability to control sexual desires so that they don't boil over into unrestrained lust. If we see our bodies as God sees them, we will have a greater respect for them. We will discipline ourselves and use our bodies the way God intended.

Throughout this book, we've told true stories of women who gave in to sexual passion. Many of these women did not save the Gift partly because they had a deep need to have their body desired and affirmed by a man. Women who are dissatisfied with their bodies need continual affirmation and reassurance that they are attractive. Listen to what Hattie, Mia, and Marisa told us:

> I guess the biggest thing that contributed to my getting involved
> sexually was that he desired me. I knew that it was not in the right

way, but I was overwhelmed because there was a man who found me attractive and he desired ME! *Hattie, age seventeen*

For me, the lure of a physical relationship is that some guy wants me, that he thinks I am beautiful. *Mia, age thirty*

I wanted to be desirable and wanted. Even when I was with this guy, I knew what I should and should not do, but I wanted to please him. And I wanted to know that I was wanted.… It made me feel good about myself. *Marisa, age twenty-one*

We can look at each of these women and easily see the error of their thinking, but when WE are the ones needing love and acceptance, the line between right and wrong can easily become blurred. How do we maintain the right attitude about our bodies? We must go to the Creator of our bodies and get His perspective about how we should view ourselves.

YOU ARE GOD'S MASTERPIECE

Out of all the women who have ever walked the face of this earth, not one has ever been just like you. God says that you are His special workmanship (Ephesians 2:10). The Greek word for workmanship in this verse is *poiema*, from which we get our English word *poem*. Did you know that you are God's poem, His masterpiece? In God's perfect plan, some poems are iambic pentameter, others haiku, some free-flowing, others a clever limerick or an ordered rhyme with a witty message. Each is unique in form and content.

The Creator of the universe intrinsically knit you together, fashioning you word upon word, line upon line until the beauty of YOU flowed out in a lyrical, poignant work of art. His loving hands formed every part of your body, making your legs just so long and turning the corners of your mouth into a smile that would make Him smile over its uniqueness. The Sovereign One molded your mind and tenderly etched certain abilities and desires within the fabric of your being. Finally, after He had gone to endless trouble and painstakingly completed the last detail, He stood back and admired His poem and said, "It is good."

Would you take a black permanent marker and scribble all over the original version of Elizabeth Barrett Browning's classic poem "How Do I Love Thee? Let Me Count the Ways"? Would you take a bucket of common tempera paint and splash it over Leonardo da Vinci's *Last Supper*? Of course not! These are works of art! Yet how often do you desecrate the masterpiece that is you by criticizing your body?

NAKED AND UNASHAMED

Lorraine: When I was in middle school, I didn't like my body. I developed early, and the boys at school called me Stuff, insinuating that I padded my bra. I was also rather chunky, and one boy in my neighborhood gave me the delightful nickname Fatty Tissue.

The summer before my sophomore year in high school, I left for three months to work at my grandparents' ranch. When I returned, my hair was longer and bleached blonde by the Nebraska sun. My thick glasses had been replaced by contacts, *and* I'd lost fifteen pounds. I was pleased with my new look until I realized that hardly anyone recognized me!

Then a disturbing thing happened. My longtime friends began to reject me, whispering behind my back and excluding me from activities. Those who had never been my friends before suddenly took a great interest in me, *especially* boys.

This deeply troubled me. Why was everyone treating me differently just because my appearance had changed? I was still the same person inside. *Who I was* had not changed. In my pain, Satan found an open door. Whenever the number on the scale inched upward, he whispered:

You are fat.

No one likes you.

You are worthless.

For years I allowed these lies to control me. One day when I was complaining to my husband, Peter, about a growing roll around my middle, he said, "Lorraine, you have a wrong view of your body, and it is hindering God's work in your life." Then he took a large black marker and wrote on a piece of white paper:

I will give thanks to You, for I am fearfully and wonderfully made. (Psalm 139:14)

Handing me the paper, he said, "I want you to tape this to the bathroom mirror. Then I want you to take off all your clothes, stand in front of the mirror, and thank God for each part of your body, beginning with the top of your head and going down to your toes."

This was NOT my idea of a good time!

Still, I knew Peter was right. So, reluctantly, I taped the verse to the bathroom mirror, took off my clothes, and looked at myself. Immediately my eyes went to the roll around my middle, and the Enemy whispered, "You are fat. No one likes you. You are worthless." *Why am I doing this? It is too painful,* I cried. But my husband's words came back to me: "Thank God for each part, beginning at the top…"

I touched the top of my head and forced my lips to say, "Thank You, God, for my hair." Once the words were out, thanking God was easier. My hair was one of my best features. I was grateful that I could start with something I liked, so with a bit more sincerity I said, "Thank You, God, for giving me lots of thick hair."

Next I looked at my eyebrows. I had never thanked God for my eyebrows before. How had God thought to put these wooly things above my eyes? And why? They seemed to serve no real purpose except to soften my face and express emotion. As I thought about it, I decided that eyebrows were pretty clever! *Thank You, God, for my eyebrows.*

My eyes were next. This one was easy. I liked the way my eyes shined when I talked about my love for the Lord and how the deep blue intensified when I laughed. I was grateful that my eyes had allowed me to witness the glorious rose-splashed sunrise earlier that morning. I closed my eyes and thought, *What would it be like not to be able to see?* I allowed myself to slip into the blackness for a moment. As I did, conviction gripped me. *What if I couldn't see the faces of my smiling children at dinner or watch the golden aspen leaves dance in the wind? What if I'd never been allowed to see a ballet or witness the surprised look on my mother's face when she opened her birthday gift?*

How had my perspective become so clouded? How could I have allowed myself to obsess over something as trivial as a few pounds of cellulite? I could see! "Forgive me, Father," I prayed. "Truly I am fearfully and wonderfully made!"

When I opened my eyes, I saw myself with *new* eyes.

With what kind of eyes do you see yourself? Do you see your body through the critical eyes of the world that says, "Your body doesn't measure up," or do you look through the eyes of your Creator who proclaims that your body is His masterpiece? Are you courageous enough to brave

God's Workmanship

You made all the delicate inner parts of my body
    and knit me together in my mother's womb.
Thank you for making me so wonderfully complex!
    Your workmanship is marvelous—and how well I know it.
You watched me as I was being formed in utter seclusion,
    as I was woven together in the dark of the womb.
You saw me before I was born.
    Every day of my life was recorded in your book.
Every moment was laid out
    before a single day had passed.
How precious are your thoughts about me, O God!
    Psalm 139:13-17 (NLT, emphasis added)

the mirror and thank God for His workmanship? We urge you to do this because it can have a profound impact on the way you see yourself.

Go before the mirror and pray:

> *God, thank You for my body. Thank You for knitting*
> *together my bones and muscles and then covering them*
> *with a soft fabric of skin. Thank You for the curves,*
> *for the beauty You poured into every cell.*
> *O God, thank You, thank You that I can walk,*
> *I can hear, I can touch and smell and see. I praise You!*
> *Truly I am fearfully and wonderfully made.*

Not only do we need to see our bodies as God sees them; we also need to control them so that we do not yield to lustful sexual appetites.

CONTROL YOUR BODY

We have both been married many years but not so many that we have forgotten the craving, the powerful pull to give in to the sexual urges coursing through our bodies. It is hard—no, that isn't strong enough—it is EXTREMELY EXCRUCIATING to try to control sexual urges, BUT it is possible.

When it comes to dealing with sexual urges, each single woman has two choices: You can choose the *path of purity* and learn to control your body, or you can give in to all that your body demands and choose the *path of passion*.

The Path of Passion

If a single woman fails to control her body and gives in to her sexual appetites, she will probably do one of three things:

- seek sexual satisfaction from another person
- masturbate
- stuff her sexual feelings

Because we devote much of the next chapter to the first response, we will address the second and third options here.

Masturbation. Nowhere in the Bible does it say, "Thou shalt not masturbate." HOWEVER (and this is a mighty big *however*), it is clear that masturbation commonly serves as a doorway to many actions the Bible clearly labels as sin. Self-pleasuring can become a dangerous addiction for many singles. The trap is easy to slip into.

> The failure came in my mind. I was lonely and needed to escape, so I read stories about people who were in a romance and pleasured myself to feel like I was somehow involved in something wonderful. *Brandie*

> I knew it was wrong to go all the way, so I turned to masturbation to satisfy my sexual feelings. At the time it felt so good. Once this became a habit, Satan inundated me with the lie that I couldn't help myself and this was the only way to deal with my strong sexual desires. *Holly*

If you are thinking, *I'd never turn to self-pleasuring,* think again. Listen to the honest words of anguish from Pam, a dynamic, single Christian leader.[2]

> For years I had a single focus—ministry for my Lord. Sexual desire was not a problem, but then…deep longings broke through the walls of what I had always considered a secure, steel box.… I found myself aching for sexual fulfillment.… Always I had trusted God to satisfy my longings, but Satan found a foothold and told me that the things I was missing should be mine.… I knew it was wrong. It was as if I was saying, "Lord, You're not satisfying my needs the way I want. I'll get them met myself." I gave my imagination full rein, creating idols and images as it would.
>
> I told myself dozens of times that the fantasizing must stop.… Yet despite all resolves, when the pressure came, I would cave in. I

realized that I was utterly powerless and that the only answer was to admit the fact and cling to the Lord.… I asked the Lord Jesus for "mercy and grace to help" in my time of need.… I realized that condemning myself and using the whip of guilt were no match for the power of temptation. Only the Lord's indwelling presence could conquer. I learned to rely on that alone.…

As I clung to Him in deep dependence, He showed me ways to escape the enticement.… He taught me to flee at the first second of mental imaging, not five seconds later at the point of no return. He was there to comfort. He was there to strengthen and help me tolerate the emptiness left by the withdrawal of satisfaction.… His tender love during those days drew my heart into an ever-deepening love for Him. It was that love that moved me, by the Spirit's power, to finally turn from the idols of my imagination.… Yes, I still fell on occasion. I still returned to the old idols in moments of empty weakness. But I hurried to confess, knowing that I would receive forgiveness and then enjoy full fellowship standing before the Father's throne—*cleansed and faultless*—dressed in the dazzling white robe of Christ's righteousness.

When we turn to self-pleasuring to satisfy sexual feelings, masturbation can become an enslaving addiction. If you suffer from this or from any sexual addiction, we recommend you seek immediate help. Ask God to show you where to go. A trained Christian counselor can prove invaluable. We also recommend the Web site *www.settingcaptivesfree.com*, which offers a free course, intensive biblical instruction, and a mentoring program for those who suffer with sexual addictions.

Stuff your sexual feelings. Women who don't want to look to self-pleasuring or to a man to gratify their desires may be tempted to stuff their sexual urges and pretend that such feelings are irrelevant or that they do not exist. This is the other extreme.

Maise didn't set out to bury her sexual feelings; it just happened.

I had a very rigid upbringing and got the impression from my mom that sex wasn't something to enjoy or talk about. My sister was boy crazy, and my parents were worried about her. I decided not to be like her and became judgmental and self-righteous about women who struggled with staying pure. I had stuffed my feelings so deeply that I was nonsensual and almost nonsexual. I'd look at women who struggled with sexual desire and think, *What's the big deal? Just say no!* My arrogant, harsh attitude affected every area of my life. When I turned thirty, I realized that my joy was gone. I felt dead inside.

While meeting with a Christian counselor, I realized the danger of my attitude. In giving up sexual feelings, I had given up pleasurable feelings and was denying who God had made me to be. The counselor encouraged me to give in to the five senses and enjoy the way they affected my body. Step by step God graciously changed me so that I could embrace my sexuality and femininity as holy and precious gifts from Him. How grateful I am that God took me on this journey of discovery before He brought my wonderful husband into my life.

We would be very grieved if any young woman after reading this book felt that the way to deal with her strong sexual urges was to stuff them and pretend they didn't exist. This is not controlling your body; it's living in denial. God desires for you to be feminine and to acknowledge your sexuality. Then you can seek God's help to control, not deny, your sexual feelings. God gives us encouragement that it *is* possible to control our bodies. Look at the exciting promise in the following passage.

The Path of Purity

We urge you in the name of the Lord Jesus to live in a way that pleases God, as we have taught you. You are doing this already, and we encourage you to do so more and more. For you remember what we taught you in the name of the Lord Jesus. God wants you to be holy, so you should keep clear of all sexual sin. Then each of you will control your body and live in holiness and honor. (1 Thessalonians 4:1-4, NLT)

The apostle Paul wrote these words, but they are exactly the words we want to say to you. So much is packed in these few verses. We see that God calls us to

• pursue purity
• keep clear of sexual sin

And if we follow the Lord's command, we will learn

• how to control our bodies
• how to live in holiness and honor

Isn't that exciting? God says that you can control your body! How? By making secret choices to follow God's path of purity. Every decision you have made as you've read this book and done the enclosed Bible study will help you to control your body. Understanding the Gift Exchange and the joy of presenting your body to your husband on your wedding night; writing your vision statement; choosing to set your heart and renew your mind—all of these choices will encourage your body to war against its surging sexual urges.

If you have stayed pure and have not had these intense desires awakened, you are blessed because the path you have chosen will make it easier to control your body. If you have given away the Gift, God forgives and makes all things new—body, soul, and spirit. But you have a problem: Your body knows too much. Your body knows the path of desire and fulfillment, so your job is to restrain your sexual desires and retrain your body, to reformat your thinking patterns and your body patterns, and to teach your body "No, I will not go down the path of desire."

You know the old myth about cold showers putting a damper on sexual desire? Cold showers never did it for either of us (besides, a cold shower is about the most excruciating form of torture known to women). So what can you do?

1. Stay at the feet of the Lord Jesus. "In thy presence is fulness of joy; at thy right hand there are pleasures for evermore" (Psalm 16:11, KJV). Spend time with Him. Listen to His voice. Pour out your heart to Him, and bask in His presence. Jesus, not a man, can be your ultimate joy and satisfaction. (Keep reading. We have MUCH to share with you in the last section of the book about this!!!)

2. Stay active and exercise your body. "I discipline my body like an athlete, training it to do what it should" (1 Corinthians 9:27, NLT). Exercise releases tension. It can also dissipate some of the hormonal symptoms that surge through your body screaming for sexual satisfaction. Run. Play tennis. Ski. Swim. Tell your body that YOU are in charge and it needs to obey you.

3. Pour yourself into the lives of others. "Do not merely look out for your own personal interests, but also for the interests of others" (Philippians 2:4). Look for opportunities to serve. When your eyes are on the needs of others, your own needs suddenly do not seem so urgent.

4. Join a discipleship program or Bible study. "Your word I have treasured in my heart, that I may not sin against You" (Psalm 119:11). Study God's Word, and think, breathe, and live God's truths. His Word will encourage you, instruct you, and take the lure out of Satan's lies.

5. Be accountable to an older woman or mentor. "Listen to counsel and accept discipline, that you may be wise the rest of your days" (Proverbs 19:20). Chose someone who is ahead of you spiritually and will "get in your face" and ask often, "How are you doing with controlling your body?" Chose someone who will ask the hard questions about masturbation.

As you make wise choices, God promises divine power for living a godly life. He has promised that you will escape the decadence all around you caused by evil desires. As you look to the Lord and trust Him, moral excellence will be added to your faith. A life of moral excellence leads to knowing God better, and knowing God better leads to self-control (2 Peter 1:3-6).

You *can* learn to be in control of your body instead of having your body control you. And you *can* accept your body and thank God that you are fearfully and wonderfully made. These two choices will take you down the path that leads to the fulfillment of your vision statement.

If we could look into your eyes right now, we believe we would see a woman of resolve, a woman who has her goal ever before her. You are on track! You have set your heart, renewed your mind, and now you are contemplating the importance of controlling your body. But you must take one more very important step: You must strengthen your will. Turn to the next chapter and discover how.

God Says to You

- ⟨⟩ I know everything about you. (Psalm 139:1-20)
- ⟨⟩ I know when you sit down and when you rise up. (Psalm 139:2)
- ⟨⟩ I am familiar with all your ways. (Psalm 139:3)
- ⟨⟩ Even the very hairs on your head are numbered. (Matthew 10:29-31)
- ⟨⟩ I created you in My image. (Genesis 1:27)
- ⟨⟩ I chose you when I planned creation. (Ephesians 1:11-12)
- ⟨⟩ I determined the exact time of your birth and where you would live. (Acts 17:26)
- ⟨⟩ You are fearfully and wonderfully made. (Psalm 139:14)
- ⟨⟩ I knit you together in your mother's womb. (Psalm 139:13)
- ⟨⟩ And brought you forth on the day you were born. (Psalm 71:6)
- ⟨⟩ It is My desire to lavish My love on you simply because you are My child. (1 John 3:1)
- ⟨⟩ I offer you more than your earthly father ever could. (Matthew 7:11)
- ⟨⟩ For I am the perfect father. (Matthew 5:48)
- ⟨⟩ Every good gift that you receive comes from My hand. (James 1:17)
- ⟨⟩ I am your provider, and I meet all your needs. (Matthew 6:31-33)
- ⟨⟩ My plan for your future has always been filled with hope. (Jeremiah 29:11)

～

- ∽ Because I love you with an everlasting love. (Jeremiah 31:3)
- ∽ My thoughts toward you are as countless as the sand on the seashore. (Psalm 139:17-18)
- ∽ And I rejoice over you with singing. (Zephaniah 3:17)
- ∽ I will never stop doing good to you. (Jeremiah 32:40)
- ∽ For you are My treasured possession. (Exodus 19:5)
- ∽ I desire to establish you with all My heart and all My soul. (Jeremiah 32:41)
- ∽ And I want to show you great and marvelous things. (Jeremiah 33:3)
- ∽ Delight in Me, and I will give you the desires of your heart. (Psalm 37:4)
- ∽ For it is I who gave you those desires. (Philippians 2:13)
- ∽ I am able to do more for you than you can possibly imagine. (Jeremiah 33:3; Ephesians 3:20)
- ∽ For I am your greatest encourager. (2 Thessalonians 2:16-17)
- ∽ I am also the Father who comforts you in all your troubles. (2 Corinthians 1:3-4)
- ∽ When you are brokenhearted, I am close to you. (Psalm 34:18)
- ∽ One day I will wipe away every tear from your eyes and take away all the pain you have suffered on this earth. (Revelation 21:3-4)
- ∽ Come home, and I'll throw the biggest party heaven has ever seen. I am waiting for you. (Luke 15:11-32)

Chapter 17

Strengthen Your Will

Taut muscles glistened in the sunlight as Marion Jones shook out her legs and placed her feet firmly in the starting blocks. Back arched, body tense, she looked like a sleek leopard ready to pounce. Her eyes stared straight ahead at the yellow tape that stretched across the finish line—her goal.

One blast of the gun, and Marion catapulted out of the blocks. Every part of her finely tuned body responded to the rhythm of speed she had trained herself to know, the speed that would now propel her to her goal. Years of gut-wrenching discipline had been given for this one golden moment.

As the American flag was hoisted high and the Olympic gold medal was placed around her neck, Marion Jones's smile reached to the skies. *I did it! The years of training, the sacrifices, every aching muscle…it was worth it!*

Remember that in a race everyone runs, but only one person gets the prize. You also must run in such a way that you will win. All athletes practice strict self-control. They do it to win a prize that will fade away, but we do it for an eternal prize. So I run straight to the goal with purpose in every step. I am not like a boxer who misses his punches. I discipline my body like an athlete, training it to do what it should. (1 Corinthians 9:24-27, NLT)

You, too, are in a race headed toward a goal—not to win a medal that will tarnish with age but to win a medal of character that will grow brighter as the years pass. You are running the race of purity. The goal line is the fulfillment of your vision statement. You have set your heart and your mind on it. You have learned to control your body. Now you must strengthen your will.

Your will is the core of who you are. It is the steel within you that exerts power or control over your actions or emotions (hence, the term "iron will"). How would you describe your will? Is it a mass of jiggling, flabby cellulite, or is it buff? Are the muscles of your will taunt and firm like those of a seasoned Olympian, or do they more closely resemble the spongy flab of a seasoned couch potato?

Perhaps your abs are in great shape, but you've never considered that your will is a muscle that needs exercise. How can you strengthen your will so that you can flee sexual passion and win the prize?

> **Flee** from anything that stimulates youthful lust. **Follow** anything that makes you want to do right. Pursue faith, love, and peace, and **Find** the companionship of those who call on the Lord with pure hearts. (2 Timothy 2:22, our emphasis and paraphrase)

Tighten your will; firm it up by repeating:
- I WILL FLEE anything that stimulates sexual passion.
- I WILL FOLLOW everything that makes me want to wait for God's timing.
- I WILL FIND friends who will encourage me to follow God's path.

Let's look in more detail at each of these three ways to strengthen your will.

"I WILL FLEE"

What does fleeing from anything that stimulates passion look like? How do you do this? To help you better understand how to flee sexual passion, we asked some young women who attended a Bible study we taught on sexual purity what they do. Here is what they said:

> *"I turn off the television if I see a sex scene developing. I saw a graphic sexual scene when I was seventeen and thought about it continually. I don't need that! I don't want any more images like this in my mind because I know where it can lead."*

> *"What helps me flee sexual passion is to pretend that God is in the room, near me and watching me."*

> *"When I'm tempted to do things I know are not right, I ask myself, 'Will I respect myself tomorrow if I do this today?'"*

> *"I am writing a journal for my future husband, and I think about what I would have to put in there if I didn't flee."*

> *"I remember that something that feels good for such a short time can leave wounds for a long time."*

> *"I have to be committed to avoid the situation before it arrives rather than trying to get out of it when I am already in the middle of it."*

> *"The most important things for me are reading the Word and knowing that God loves me so that I don't need sexual stuff to fill a love void in my life."*

> *"I have to control what I watch, read, or listen to. No one can do that but me."*

This last point is crucial for anyone who wants to remain sexually pure. What do you watch, read, and listen to? Different things stimulate women in different ways. We know one young woman who doesn't watch movies or read certain novels because of how they can trigger sexual passion in her. Are we suggesting that you not go to movies? No, we are not making recommendations. Our goal is to get you to think and to challenge you to be serious with God. He says:

- Turn your eyes away from anything impure. "I will set before my eyes no vile thing." (Psalm 101:3, NIV)

- Turn your ears away from anything impure. "Obscene stories, foolish talk, and coarse jokes—these are not for you." (Ephesians 5:4, NLT)

Will you ask God, "What does it mean for me to turn my eyes and ears away from anything impure?"

The second way to strengthen our wills is to *follow* anything that makes us want to wait for God's timing.

"I WILL FOLLOW"

The Greek word for *follow* has the idea of pursuing with all your energy. Marion Jones won a gold medal because she set her will and then ran with all her energy straight toward that goal. What kept her from running off course? Her lane lines. If she had ignored these boundaries, Marion would have lost the medal.

Boundaries will also help you run straight toward the goal of your vision statement. Let us recommend three boundaries that can help you keep on track with your goal of purity.

Set a Boundary on Dress
God doesn't mince words:

> I want women to be modest in their appearance. They should wear decent and appropriate clothing and not draw attention to themselves. (1 Timothy 2:9, NLT)

Certain boundaries of modesty are universal; others will be personalized according to cultural environment and how God made you. If you are big on the top, you must be careful about wearing things that are low cut or fit tightly across the front. If you have long, shapely legs, your boundary may be not to wear extremely short shorts. It is important to take into account how God created you and also to remember how God created your Christian brothers. Guys are aroused by what they see—they respond to a woman's soft, shapely form. Maybe you know this in your head, but are you considering how your appearance affects men? One young man comments, "Man, doesn't she get it? Doesn't she know that her skimpy top gives me hours of agony?"

Based on 1 Timothy 2:9, good questions to ask yourself would be
• Do I dress modestly?
• Do I dress appropriately?
• Do I draw attention to myself by the way I dress?
We asked single women to share some of their boundaries on dress.

God has shown me that any bit of breasts, stomach, or bottom gives a guy things to think about that takes his mind places it shouldn't go. *Robin*

Nothing too tight or too short and no midriffs. Basically, nothing that will draw attention to parts of my body that guys like. *Rachel*

I believe God wants my dress to be the same whether I'm with my boyfriend or with my parents or pastor. *Stephanie*

We challenge you: Will you set a boundary on dress?

Set a Boundary on Time
Of course you need to spend time with someone in order to get to know him, but you also need to be wise about how much togetherness is appropriate. For example, do *not* go for an all-day hike into the woods alone with the one you love. Instead, take an afternoon walk, and invite an army of friends to accompany you. Do *not* go to his apartment where the two of you will be alone until the wee hours of the morning. If you go to his apartment, are you really going to just play Trivial Pursuit—or are you hoping deep down that the game will end in something not so trivial?

Where was my brain anyway? What was I thinking? What did I think would happen lying side by side in front of the blazing fire? After two hours of shared confidences, passionate looks, too many kisses, and too much body contact, I was the one on fire. Not to mention Jon. And then I said, "No." Why did I let it get to that point? I feel so mean.... We just can't be alone like that because I'm afraid the next time I won't say, "No." *Janey*

We asked single women about time boundaries that had worked for them. Here is what they said:

- Create specific date nights so that you aren't spending every waking moment together.
- Date in groups—this limits alone time.
- Limit late-night phone calls.
- Limit the lateness of a date. (When you're tired, your defenses are down.)

We challenge you: Will you set a boundary on time?

Set a Boundary on Touch

We want to help you establish your personal touch boundaries, but first let us ask you two questions that can influence the boundaries you set.

1. Are you a wall or a door? In the Song of Solomon, the young bride's brothers ask whether their sister is a wall or a door.

If she is a wall, we will build on her a battlement of silver; but if she is a door, we will barricade her with planks of cedar. (Song of Solomon 8:9)

A wall is a young woman who fortifies herself with God's Word against the surging desires within and sets firm boundaries on touch. A door is a young woman who lacks boundaries on touch. She is easily accessible and opens herself to sexual pleasures outside of marriage.

The young bride was a wall. Have you been a wall or a door in your relationships with men?

2. *Do you have a positive relationship with your father?* According to Kevin Leman, "The father-daughter relationship is the key to every woman's aching heart. It's the genesis of every grown woman's sighs. It's also, unfortunately, the missing ingredient in many lost souls."[1] Young women from a home where the father figure is absent may become sexually promiscuous in a search for a man's affection.[2]

> My father never paid much attention to me, so I think I gave in to being physical with my boyfriend because I wanted love and value from guys. *Kami*

Both of us can identify with Kami's comment.

Lorraine: My father was killed in a plane crash when I was seven. Because there was a void of male affection when I was little, I found myself trying to satisfy that void in unhealthy ways later on, like scheduling four different dates on the same day so I'd get hugs from four different guys.

Linda: My father was an alcoholic and uninvolved with me. I had steady boyfriends from the time I was thirteen. I always wore a guy's ring around my neck, a sorority pin, or an engagement ring—anything that validated me and said, "You are loved."

We both wish this book had been written when we were dating, because it would have encouraged us to have boundaries in the area of touch. We didn't realize until many years after we were married that our lack of relationship with our fathers had influenced our desire for touch. Just as an absent father can have a negative influence on a young woman's sexual choices, so a strong father-daughter relationship can be a positive influence.

> Dad was my biggest fan. His love for me made me feel beautiful and accepted. I never craved attention from guys like some of my friends and finally decided it was because I was Daddy's little sweetheart. *Tish*

Your answers to these two questions will affect the specific boundaries you need to make about touch. God commands us to flee what hinders and follow what helps (2 Timothy 2:22). He asks us to run away from anything that stimulates sexual passion. What stimulates sexual passion in you?

Josh McDowell in his book *Why Wait?* says that 65 percent of Christian singles are involved in oral sex. They feel this is not "real sex" because they are not breaking the intercourse barrier.

Think, our friend, think! Heavy petting, hours of everything but intercourse is NOT, we repeat NOT, fleeing sexual passion. Do not be deceived! Such activity is running headfirst into "youthful lusts." Any activity that stimulates sexual passion in you or the person you are with is NOT God's best for you.

We are not trying to be your bodyguard (pun intended!) and set your limits for you. You have to set your own limits, because only you know your weaknesses and personal vulnerabilities. But we want you to be honest and to think about where your choices in the area of touch can lead. For instance:

Does bare chest against bare breasts help you flee or follow?

Does heavy petting help you flee or follow?

Does oral sex help you flee or follow?

We think you'll agree that such sexual activities push any single woman straight into the arms of sexual passion.

Here are a few more questions. These may be more difficult to answer.

Does French kissing help you flee or follow?

Does a sensuous backrub help you flee or follow?

Does close hugging help you flee or follow?

Only you know the answers for *you*. Tuck 2 Timothy 2:22 away in your heart and mind, and next time you aren't sure about something you and your boyfriend/fiancé are doing, ask yourself:

Does this help me **flee** sexual passion?

Does this help me **follow** God's plan?

We challenge you: Will you set a boundary on touch?

Now we're ready for the third exercise for strengthening the will:

"I WILL FIND"

Stop for a moment and think about your close friendships. Do your friends know God and follow hard after Him? Is the desire of their hearts to walk His path of purity? We cannot stress enough how important it is that you find friends who will help you as you follow God's path. The road is often long and hard, and you need encouragement along the way.

> Be prepared. You're up against far more than you can handle on your own. Take all the help you can get. (Ephesians 6:12-13, MSG)

You need help in this race of purity from your family, friends, and church leaders. The life of Moses gives us a beautiful picture of how family and friends can help us when we are in trouble or need assistance. Israel was in a battle with the Amalekites, and God had asked Moses to stand on the top of the hill and hold his hands high all day. As long as Moses held up his hands, the Israelites were winning, but whenever he lowered his hands, the Amalekites got the upper hand. But Moses' arms grew tired, so his brother, Aaron, and his friend Hur sat Moses on a rock and came behind him and held his arms up, one on each side, and Israel won the battle (Exodus 17:12-13).

The giant redwood trees in California also illustrate the strength we can gain from others. These majestic trees that stretch to the heavens take our breath away. But a redwood tree cannot stand alone. Redwoods grow in groves because they need the roots of their neighbors in order to stay upright. These intertwined roots hold up the entire forest.

Find people who will help to strengthen your will to stay on God's path of purity.

Pray:

Lord, help me find a friend who will hold my hands up.

Mighty God, lead me to an older, godly woman who will hold me
accountable and encourage me as I walk Your path of purity.
Father, show me whose hands I can hold up
so they can also flee sexual passion.

God cares deeply about this race of purity you are running. He understands the importance of having an iron will to help you to stay on track. He longs for your vision statement to become a reality. He does not send you out to run this important race alone; He offers His Holy Spirit as your personal trainer. The Spirit of God will teach you what you need to know and help strengthen your will so that you are fit for the race.

Each purposeful choice to *flee, follow,* and *find* strengthens the muscles of your will, but do not think that you grunt through these workouts with no joy. Quite the opposite! Each action you take infuses joy into your soul because, in your obedience, you delight the heart of God. Each choice to save and protect the Gift is not just about honoring your future husband or having the perfect wedding day and honeymoon. Your choices go deeper and have a higher purpose. They are literally acts of worship to God.

Your Act of Worship

"Wait a minute, Linda and Lorraine, isn't worship about singing praise songs?" Yes, we worship God when we lift our voice in praise, but we *also* worship Him when we make choices that please Him.

Each step you take to save the Gift brings glory to the Holy One. Each choice to save the Gift is as a song of praise—an offering—to Him. Oh, how your heavenly Father rejoices, reaching out with delight to accept your offering of praise.

The night you said no and walked away, He received worship.

The day you said good-bye to the guy whose values were not yours, He received worship.

The afternoon you cried because waiting was agony, but you kept your resolve, He received worship.

We've stressed the need to strengthen your will. Will you do that now? Won't you ask God to give you the conviction to say:

- I WILL FLEE anything that stimulates sexual passion.
- I WILL FOLLOW everything that makes me want to wait for Your timing.
- I WILL FIND friends who will encourage me to follow Your path.

As you take each of these steps, you are becoming more and more the woman you wrote about in your vision statement, and you are increasing the likelihood that you will meet your goal. God delights in each step you take. One day you will say, "It was worth every sacrifice, every aching muscle. It was worth it!"

Guarding the Gift

Come, daughter.
Rest in My arms; sink down into the
quietness of My love.
I want you to know
How much I care.
How much I delight in you.
How pleased I am with the steps you
are taking to follow Me.
But, child, be warned—your decision
angers My enemy. Because you
love Me. . .
he wants to harm you.
He intends to steal the Gift.
He seeks to separate you from Me.

My enemy is evil. . .crafty. . .strong.
But take courage, dear one.
I am stronger than he.

Trust Me. Remain in My love. And
victory
will
be
ours.

Chapter 18

Monique: One Woman's Testimony

Hi. My name is Monique. I need to tell you something, something I wish someone had told me. If only I'd been more alert, if only someone had grabbed me by the shoulders and screamed in my face, "Monique, WAKE UP!" things might have been different.

But that didn't happen, and I made mistakes—big ones.

My parents raised me to believe in God. When I was thirteen, I went to a conference on sexual purity and made a commitment to wait for sex until marriage. The words were easy to say because, back then, boys were the last thing on my mind. But by the time I was a senior in high school, being with a boy was all I could think about. A battle raged in my body. I assumed that the battle was *physical*—a struggle with my hormones. The idea that I was involved in a *spiritual* battle never occurred to me.

I knew that the Bible called Satan a tempter and a thief and that he was God's enemy. But I never thought of him as *my* enemy. Why should he bother with me? It's not like I'm important or anything.

I realize now that I opened myself up to temptation by reading steamy romance novels and watching movies with graphic sex scenes. Satan used these mental images to chip away at my commitment to sexual purity.

Don't get me wrong, *I take full responsibility for my wrong choices,* but I foolishly discounted Satan and the fact that I was in a spiritual battle for my purity. By the time I woke up and realized this, Satan was dancing at his victory party.

You may be tempted to dismiss what I am saying, thinking that I'm one of those who blames Satan for everything. That is just what Satan wants you to think. If you are busy thinking about *me,* you won't think about *him*—that he is real and that he has an army of demons ready to do his bidding.

Do not be ignorant of the devil's schemes, the Bible warns.[1] I was ignorant five years ago—I'm not today. I'm sharing my story with you because I don't want you—or anyone else—to go through the pain I've gone through. If I can show you how I was deceived, maybe you won't make the same mistakes I did.

~⁓

My stomach fluttered expectantly. It was my senior prom, and I was determined that this would be the most memorable night of my life.

I made my grand entrance down the staircase, smiling at my adoring public (Mom, Dad, and Leslie, my little sis).

"Oh, Monique, you look like a princess," my mom whispered through tears as she brushed a loose thread off my dress. My hair was a work of art. The emerald drop earrings brought out the green in my eyes. The dress was perfect—sleek and bare. I felt so sophisticated.

Dad snapped a picture, momentarily blinding me. "Where did my baby girl go?" he sighed from behind the lens.

The doorbell rang. Leslie clutched her kitty, Oreo, in one hand and opened the door with the other. Her eyes grew wide, and her mouth dropped open.

"Wow, Aaron! You look *different,*" Leslie gushed.

For once, my little sister was right. Outfitted in a regal black tux, my boyfriend had been transformed into a dashing prince bearing gifts. My heart leaped as our eyes met.

His admiring gaze lingered on the bare skin of my shoulders and on the tight fit of my dress. Walking toward me, he held out a delicate baby orchid. "This is for you, Monique," he smiled.

My heart raced as he touched my bare skin, fumbling to pin the corsage to my dress. I was glad when my mom rushed to his rescue. "Let me help with that, dear."

As Aaron and I walked arm in arm toward the car, Dad hollered, "Aaron, you treat my little girl good, you hear?" What he really meant was, "Keep your hands off her, or I will come after you with a shotgun."

Aaron laughed. "I promise to take *very* good care of her, sir." What he meant was, "Just wait till I get her alone, and I'll give her a kiss that will make her head spin."

As he started the car, Aaron looked at me with eyes that drank me in, and he asked, "Ready for our big night?"

Warmth rushed through my body as desire filled me. "I'm ready," I said, far more confidently than I felt.

⌒

My body tingled in anticipation as Aaron steered the car north on Highway 30. We had danced, laughed, and hung out with friends. Now we were alone. My emotions flip-flopped between eagerness and reluctance about where we were headed. The senior breakfast would not start for three hours. Three hours was a long time...

Several couples from our class announced to everyone that they were headed to motel rooms after the dance. We would never do anything so blatant, but even now we were headed to a place where we could be alone.

As we drove, a conflict raged in my heart and mind. *Remember your promise to your parents... Don't be a prude... Be careful... Remember how good his touch felt last time you were together.* Push, pull. Back and forth. I turned up the radio to drown out my thoughts.

Aaron chatted away. He talked about Becky and Kurt and whether they'd ever get back together after the nasty argument they had on the dance floor. As we passed the McGreggors' place, he commented on their new horse barn. He rattled on about whether they'd have sausage or pancakes or both at the breakfast. I could tell he was nervous—and that made me even more excited, because I knew what he was thinking...

As he turned left onto the dirt road that led to the old Swanson farm, our conversation also took a turn.

"You were the prettiest girl there tonight, Monique."

"I had to be—otherwise you'd have shown me up," I teased.

"No, I mean it. I've never seen you look more beautiful."

He pulled up under the familiar oak tree next to an abandoned shed and shut off the car lights. The moon was full.

He slid a CD into the player and selected *our* song. The moment I heard the first melodic piano strains, warmth surged through me, melting my resistance and filling me with an indescribable yearning.

"Cold?" he asked.

"A little."

"Your dress is a knockout, but it doesn't cover you up. Why don't we get into the backseat, and I'll put my arms around you and keep you warm?"

When we got into the back of the car, he pulled me to himself, and I inhaled the strong scent of him. It felt good to have him so near.

I lifted my chin. He lowered his head, covering my lips with his—softly at first, then with mounting hunger.

He kissed my mouth. My neck. My bare shoulders.

The hand that rested on my knee inched slowly upward. Three songs later, the car windows were steamed up, and so were we.

One part of me screamed, "More!" Another part shouted, "Stop!" The battle between God and Satan was taking place in my own heart; my body, will, and mind were all involved, each wanting different things. The voice of darkness and the voice of light argued within me:

It's okay to do this. You love each other.

Stop! You are in danger.

What's the big deal? You've gone farther than this before and were able to stop.

Go any farther, and there is no turning back.

The song playing on the CD player reinforced the "let yourself go" message with its seductive plea, "Let me love you tonight." Oh how I wanted to be able to do that—I didn't want to wait! As Aaron's body pressed into mine, I melted into him, allowing every part of my being to tell him the words I couldn't bring myself to say.

Just then a still voice whispered, *Monique, remember your promise to God.*

"Maybe we should slow down, Aaron."

"I love you, Monique. You know that."

"I love you too, Aaron. But we're going too far, and you know I want to save myself for the man I marry—"

He pressed into forbidden territory. His husky whisper undid me. "Maybe I'll be that man."

The thief was waiting. He took what he was after, and then he was gone.

~

A million times I've wished I could go back to that night and make different choices. Aaron and I broke up three months later, and the regret I feel over giving away the most intimate part of me kills me.

What I was certain was love, what I imagined would last forever was just passing infatuation. I know now that God wasn't being mean by asking me to wait for sexual intimacy until I got married. He wanted my best. He wanted to protect me. But I wouldn't listen.

But if you'll listen, at least some good will come of my pain.

Please, please, for your own good. Listen to God's voice, not Satan's. Then, unlike me, you won't have regrets.

~

Love is...	Lust is...
Love is patient.	Lust is demanding.
Love is kind	Lust is cruel
and is not jealous.	and is often jealous.
Love does not brag	Lust boasts
and is not arrogant.	and is proud of conquests.
Love does not act unbecomingly.	Lust is rude.
It does not seek its own	It cares nothing for others
and is not provoked.	and is easily stirred to anger.
Love bears all things,	Lust is self-centered.
believes all things,	It sees what it wants,
hopes all things,	pursues what it wants,
endures all things.	takes what it wants.
Love never fails.	Lust is never satisfied.

* Based on 1 Corinthians 13:4-8

Chapter 19

Satan's Lies

In *The Screwtape Letters,* C. S. Lewis writes:

> There are two equal and opposite errors into which our race can fall
> about the devils. One is to disbelieve in their existence. The other is
> to believe, and to feel an excessive and unhealthy interest in them.[1]

Satan is alive and active on planet earth, of this we are convinced. Neither of us is given to seeing demons around every corner, but as we travel around the country, we have seen firsthand the intensification of demonic activity aimed at robbing men and women of sexual purity.

We know that Satan is only one of many factors that can influence a young woman's decision to engage in premarital sex. But with each hurting woman we console, our anger at Satan escalates. We hate Satan's conniving schemes, his evil, vile ways. We despise his deceptions and his destructive lies. When we weep with a woman who has been deeply wounded to the core of her sexuality, we want to yell at him, "GET OUT OF HERE, AND LEAVE GOD'S DAUGHTERS ALONE!"

Satan has remained hidden in the bushes far too long. It's time to expose him. It's time to wise up to his schemes. It's time to rise up in spiritual authority and win back for God what Satan has stolen.

Satan knows that the Gift is important to each young woman and to God. He seeks to steal the Gift by perverting truth and speaking his native language, the language of lies. He did this with Monique. He will try to do it with you. Let's refute three lies that you can expect Satan to hurl at you.

1. Satan's Lie: "I'm Just a Harmless Halloween Character"

Satan says, "Yes! Believe that I'm a dirty old man in a red suit, holding a pitchfork. Don't take me seriously. Only very fanatical or eccentric people believe I am a real person."

Many believe this lie. According to a recent survey, 47 percent of *born-again Christians* believe that Satan is merely a symbol of evil, *not* a living being.[2]

God's Truth: "Satan is a real person of infinite evil."

God tells us that Satan is a powerful angel who fell from favor because he sought to be God's equal. When God banished him from His dwelling place, Satan took a third of the angels with him. These fallen angels, called demons, serve Satan by continually implementing planned activities to thwart God's purposes and to cause alienation between God and His people (Isaiah 14:12; Ezekiel 28:12-17).

Satan's name means *adversary.*[3] An adversary is an "enemy, a foe, or a person having hostility for another person."[4] The very name *Satan* tells us that he is hostile toward God and toward those who love God. *Devil* means *slanderer.*[5] A slanderer is someone who utters a malicious report or who tries to injure the reputation of another.[6] The very name *Devil* warns us that he is out to harm our reputations—and God's reputation.

People's titles can reveal as much about them as their names. Jesus' titles are Wonderful Counselor, Mighty God, Everlasting Father, Prince of Peace (Isaiah 9:6). Satan's titles, in contrast, are Evil One (1 John 5:19) and Tempter (1 Thessalonians 3:5).

Satan's titles and names are frightening, but there is more. His rap sheet reads like this:

He is a murderer (John 8:44).

He is a liar (John 8:44).

He is an accuser (Revelation 12:10).

He is an adversary (1 Peter 5:8).

He is a deceiver (Genesis 3:13).

No wonder Satan wants us to believe that he is a harmless Halloween figure! If we believe his lie, we won't take him seriously, and it will make it easier for him to accomplish his goal—to destroy us.

2. Satan's Lie: "God Withholds Good from You"

Satan came to Eve in the Garden of Eden and said, "God does not want you to eat from the Tree of Knowledge of Good and Evil because then you will become wise, just like God" (see Genesis 3:1-5). Satan's goal was to get Eve to question God's intentions toward her. By implication, Satan was saying, "God is unfair. He is withholding something good from you. If He really loved you, He would let you eat *any* fruit you want *anytime* you want." As Eve held the fruit in her hand, Satan prodded, "Go for it, Evie. Touch it. Feel it. Take a big bite. Nothing bad will happen."

Just as the evil one came to Eve, he comes to you and whispers, "God is unfair. He is withholding sex from you. He doesn't have your best in mind. If He did, He would let you enjoy sex *any* time with *anyone* you want. Go ahead. Touch, feel, enjoy. Nothing bad will happen."

Do you see the lies?

- If God loved you, He wouldn't withhold sex from you.
- If God loved you, He'd let you satisfy your desires.
- If God loved you, He wouldn't make you wait.

God's Truth: "God wants your best."

God loved Eve. He knew that if she ate the fruit He had forbidden, she would ultimately be the loser. She would lose intimate fellowship with God. She would lose her precious innocence. She would bite into something too big to handle.

Do you see the truth?

- Because God loves you, He created a wonderful Gift for you to enjoy—in marriage.
- Because God loves you, He asks you to refrain from doing things that will harm you.
- Because God loves you, He asks you to wait for the right time to open the Gift.

If you bite into the apple of sexual desire before marriage, you will bite into something too big for you to handle. Your loving Father created you for an intimate oneness that He wants you to have *with your husband.* God wrapped the tempting treat of sexual pleasure in the bonds of marriage because He knew that deep, physical intimacy must be experienced within the context of a lifetime commitment. The truth is: *God wants you to wait for sex because He wants your best.*

3. Satan's Lie: "There Is No Battle"

Satan says, "All this talk about a spiritual war is ridiculous. How can there be a battle when you can't even see it?"

One college girl wrote:

My commitment to sexual purity is a decision I make; no one influences that decision but me. I'm a realist. The idea that God and Satan are fighting over my sexual purity or that somehow good and evil angels are involved in this is straight out of a science fiction novel. I just don't buy it.

God's Truth: "An ongoing battle between good and evil rages all around you."

God says, "For we are not fighting against people made of flesh and blood, but against the *evil rulers* and *authorities of the unseen world,* against *those mighty powers of darkness* who rule this world, and against *wicked spirits* in the heavenly realms" (Ephesians 6:12, NLT, emphasis added).

We live in two realms: the physical realm, which we can see, and the spiritual realm, which we can't see. Battles are fought in both places. A physical battle that takes place on foreign soil may not affect us, but the spiritual battle always affects us because, while the battle is fought in the heavenlies, it is also fought in our mind. The spiritual battle involves us, and it involves angels. The Lord's angels fight *for us* because God loves us; Satan's angels fight *against us* because he hates us.

You've likely witnessed the fallout from this battle. You've seen firsthand the pain, the emptiness, the evil done at Satan's bidding. Maybe you've cried with a friend as she wept bitterly that she gave the Gift to someone who "loved her and left her." Perhaps you've heard the anguish in the voice of a classmate or coworker as she described how the Gift was taken from her by force. You may know someone who has been "used" sexually by others, and the vacant, empty look in her eyes makes your heart ache.

Unless we believe that we have an adversary who lies, tempts, and accuses, we won't be prepared for the attacks of our enemy. Like Monique, we will end up being a casualty of a war that we didn't even realize existed.

What about you? Do you believe a spiritual battle exists over your commitment to sexual purity? Perhaps you haven't thought much about this until now, but you are beginning to see that this could be true. Still, you have questions. How can we fight an enemy we cannot see? Can we do anything that will help us become more aware of this spiritual battle?

Yes, we can pray and ask God to open our eyes.

Second Kings tells the story of how prayer opened one man's eyes to the spiritual battle. King Aram was angry with Elisha, God's prophet, so he sent his soldiers to capture him. The king's warriors surrounded the village where Elisha and his servant were staying, and when the servant saw the army about to descend, he cried, "Oh, my lord, what shall we do?"

> "Don't be afraid," the prophet answered. "Those who are with us
> are more than those who are with them."
> And Elisha prayed, "O LORD, open his eyes so he may see."
> Then the LORD opened the servant's eyes, and he looked and
> saw the hills full of horses and chariots of fire all around Elisha.
> (2 Kings 6:16-17, NIV)

Elisha's words are the very words we would use to encourage you. First, *don't be afraid.* Yes, Satan has an army, but his power is miniscule compared to God's. God is eager to protect you and fight on your behalf.

Second—and we cannot stress this enough—*it is vital that you acknowledge the spiritual battle over your sexual purity.* Many women are afraid to think about Satan because they fear it will make them more vulnerable to his attacks, as if being enlightened about spiritual warfare somehow invites demonic influence. This is another one of Satan's lies! The woman who acknowledges the battle can fight with confidence in the Lord, but the one who denies the battle becomes an easy target for the Enemy.

God is our great warrior. He is mighty to save. We need never fear Satan because our trust and hope is in the King of kings and Lord of lords. Even so, God wants us to be actively involved in the battle because our participation blesses us and glorifies Him. Won't you ask God to open your eyes to the battle so that you are not ignorant of the devil's schemes (2 Corinthians 2:11)?

> *Lord, open my eyes so that I may see the battle*
> *over my sexual purity. Help me to rest in the truth*
> *that Your forces outnumber the forces of the Enemy*
> *and that when I am in need,*
> *Your help is only a prayer away.*
> *I love You, Father. Thank You for loving me.*
> *Thank You that I need never fear,*
> *because You are my protector.*

Chapter 20

The Lure of the Tempter

Any understanding of Satan must begin with this important fact: *Satan is* not *the opposite of God.*

God is the Creator; Satan is a created being. God is omnipotent; Satan has limited knowledge. God is omnipresent; Satan is bound by time and space. Satan has powers, but he is not all-powerful. He is the commander of an army of demons whose primary goal is to thwart the plans of God and destroy those who serve Him. When we say that Satan is out to destroy you and to steal the Gift, we are not implying that Satan himself is always the one doing this, but rather the organization that represents him and ultimately carries out his will.

Satan leads a hierarchy of fallen angels who have assigned dominions and specialized skills, a counterfeit copy of God's order of created beings (Ezekiel 28:11-14; Isaiah 14:12-14; Ephesians 6:12). We can well imagine Satan instructing one of his demons with a letter like this:

To Dameon, Special Agent, Division of Sexual Deception:

Your commission to add to my storehouses the "treasures" of virgins is a most high honor. Study your assignment's personality and inclinations carefully before you calculate the time, place, and means by which you will appropriate her treasure.

Deceive her about the true value of her virginity. Use every opportunity to suggest that waiting is archaic, and that virginity is to be disdained rather than prized. Implant these thoughts into her mind on a regular basis:

Go ahead, everyone is doing it.

God gave you these sexual desires; He wants you to express them.

We love each other, so it must be okay.

Flood her mind with images and messages that undermine her commitment to sexual purity. Use romance novels, sexually explicit movies, MTV, billboards, the Internet—anything that will ignite sexual passion in her. Once the images are in her mind, luring her across the line into action is child's play.

Remember, Dameon, you must not let her converse with the Enemy. DO encourage her to attend church functions that focus on superficial instruction or social activities so that she will develop a false sense of religious devotion, but DO NOT let her pray to the Enemy or read His Word. Above all, Dameon, see to this or all will be lost.

If you are clever and consistent, the ease with which your assignment gives away her treasure will delight and amuse you. I offer all my resources to ensure your victory.

Your Exalted Leader,

Satan

Women instinctively understand that their virginity has value and significance. No woman gives away the Gift without some forethought. Rather, she is enticed to do so through a series of choices bound within a process called temptation. If you are to be victorious in your commitment to save the Gift, you must understand the process of temptation and the tempter's role in it.

The Process of Temptation

According to Webster's dictionary, *temptation* is the process by which a person is enticed to do wrong through pleasure or gain. God wants us to understand that temptation is a strong pull that entices us away from godly thinking and pushes us into sinful actions. Temptation has a beginning (the initial enticement), an end (death), and several steps in between. In Scripture it is clear that each step builds upon the previous one:

> Each one is *tempted* when, by his own evil desire, he is dragged away and *enticed*. Then, after desire has conceived, it gives birth to sin; and sin, when it is full-grown, gives birth to *death*. (James 1:14-15, NIV, emphasis added)

Let us give you three words that will make the process of temptation clearer: temptation, contemplation, and activation.

Temptation: Being tempted is not a sin, but the moment a tempting sexual thought or situation presents itself, you must make a decision by saying: "No, I will not go there," or, "Yes, this is something to consider." If you say no, you have resisted temptation. You have not sinned.

Contemplation: But if you say, "Yes, I'll consider this," you then begin to contemplate, and suddenly your mind goes wild with possibilities. This is where sin begins.

Activation: Continued contemplation in your mind causes your body to activate, and you commit the sin that results in death.

The death described in James 1:15 is not physical death but spiritual and emotional death—a death of innocence, intimacy with God, or the death of your dream of sexual purity.

If you are not currently facing sexual temptation, you will. Temptation is common to all of us:

> No temptation has seized you except what is common to man. And God is faithful; he will not let you be tempted beyond what you can bear. But when you are tempted, he will also provide a way out so that you can stand up under it. (1 Corinthians 10:13, NIV)

You will find it easier to resist temptation if you understand the tempter's part in it and the ways that God makes escape possible.

Hallway of Temptation

Imagine a long hallway stretching before you, the Hallway of Temptation. It is an unusual hallway with windows along one side. Light fills the entrance. Here the window is actually a large sliding glass door with a handle that you can pull for a quick exit. But as you progress down the hall, the windows become increasingly smaller and higher, making escape more difficult. At the very end of the hall, the windows are tiny slits close to the ceiling. It would take a ladder and a skinny body to squeeze through the final window of escape.

The carpet on the floor of the hallway is worn; obviously many people have traveled these corridors. A bright yellow line labeled Contemplation is painted on the floor past the first window. At the end of the hall is a door labeled Activation. Satan stands in the doorway and eagerly motions for you to come. "Hurry!" he urges. "You are missing all the excitement!" It appears he is right, for just beyond him is a room filled with people who all seem to be having a roaringly good time.

Earlier you met Monique, who gave away the Gift to Aaron after her senior prom. Let's consider her progression down the Hallway of Temptation.

In the early stages of dating, Monique watched television and witnessed a couple in bed together, kissing and touching. The thought entered her mind, *I wonder what it would be like to be in bed with Aaron.* This thought placed her at the entrance of the Hallway of Temptation. At that moment she could have quickly escaped through the first sliding glass door by rejecting the thought and clicking off the television. If she had done this, she would have resisted temptation, and she would not have sinned.

Instead of saying no to the thought, Monique pondered it. She imagined how it would feel to have Aaron lying naked beside her. In doing this, she walked past the first window of escape. She crossed the yellow line on the floor labeled Contemplation. Monique was in sin.[1]

She continued to contemplate as she read steamy romance novels. In her mind, Aaron and she replaced the images of the characters in the story making love. She imagined what it would be like to have his hands roaming over her body. With each thought, she journeyed farther down the hallway. With each step, the windows of escape became smaller. Satan was closer now, and the revelry in the room at the end of the hall grew more enticing. Under the doorway of Activation, Satan wooed, "Come join us, Monique. This is where you want to be."

By the time Monique and Aaron were parked at the Swanson farm, she was already near the door of Activation. Only a few windows of escape remained. What had been inconceivable as she stood at the entrance of the hallway now seemed quite plausible. As their kisses grew more passionate, God pointed to a window of escape, but Monique ignored His voice and listened instead to the voice of Satan.

Monique walked through the door of Activation. Satan's party was not what the tempter had promised. All the laughter and fun had been concentrated around the doorway entrance. Once inside the room, Monique discovered that guilt and shame consumed most of the people. They shook their fists at the tempter, angry at his deception. Monique, too, was angry, and she spent her days relentlessly searching for a way out of the room.

Where are you? If you have said no to temptation and jumped out the sliding door, we thank God and applaud your decision. If you have crossed over the yellow line of Contemplation and are walking toward Activation, we plead with you: STOP! WAKE UP! Do not be deceived. We beg you in the name of the Lord Jesus Christ, climb out through the first window you see and escape the hallway that leads to death. If you have already walked through the doorway of Activation, even here there is a way of escape, a way of hope—and Monique found it.

Jesus is the way (John 14:6). He is the door (John 10:7). In Jesus, there is forgiveness. In Jesus, there is always hope for a new beginning (see chapter 9, "Cutting the Ties of Sexual Sin").

The Lord does not want us to be ignorant about the tempter and his ways. He wants us to embrace the truth that the battle for sexual purity is not just a *physical* battle but a *spiritual* battle. But praise God, we do not have to fight this battle alone. God fights with us. And He gives us some very creative spiritual weapons to use against Satan. Let's look in the next chapter at three of these weapons and see how they can be used to battle our enemy.

Cover Me with Dignity
by Jean Huggins

I thought there was no danger. I thought that I was tough—
A rare and priceless diamond, not a diamond in the rough.
I'd be just friends when dating men for that's the way to start—
Open to the chance of love—but God would guard my heart.
He'd spread a cover over me with His mighty wings.
I'd snuggle in the safety of my tender, loving King.

No man could ever touch my heart the way that my God can.
The world could not pull me apart—until I met this man.
He stepped into my life one night, quite intriguingly.
A man? A snake? A devil? I'd say he was all three.
And yet this man's so charming. Of course, I knew his game.
But I was well protected, so closer still I came.

This snake began to craft his work, so very clandestine.
His argument, fine sounding, a smooth and potent wine.
But the tenderness he offered was only counterfeit.
He pulled me into his strong arms and lured me down the pit.
Less of God, more of him, an idol substitute.
He spread a cover over me, a snare to steal my fruit.

So just as Eve, I was deceived with all of Satan's cunning.
Sincere and pure devotion strayed; I knew I should be running.
He whispered softly in my ear; deceit he did express.
"Let's deepen our relationship toward the ultimate caress."
His flesh extended over me. "I care for you, my dear."
I knew the truth yet still hung on—what did I have to fear?

Yet fear I did—for lies he spoke—no longer in denial.
This was not an act of love, but only to defile.
His venom did not enter me, pride leads me to confess.
I slipped away and closed the door, but too late nonetheless.
Now I lay me down to sleep, naked, bruised with shame,
For now I have no covering, no dignity to claim.

So here I am, God, in the raw, wounded to the core.
Embarrassed, lost, and beaten down, I could hurt no more.
I placed a man in high esteem; the idol was so wrong.
My heart weeps and thirsts for You, for only You belong.
You're the God who chooses me no matter what I do.
Forgive me, Lord. Please cleanse my heart. I know that I've hurt
    You.

I heard You are a jealous God, and now I know just why.
Why would I long for such abuse when You can make me fly?
I'll walk with You. I'll dance with You. I'll seek You with my heart.
I must go through the pain, I know, but still I want to start.
Will You cover me with dignity? Will You clean up all the shame?
Will You crush the lack of high regard—put purity in my name?

"My daughter, I will cover you. I'll clothe you like a queen.
With dignity and honor, wrap you up in high esteem.
I'll cover you with kindness. I will look upon your face.
My fragrance lingers over you. I'll tuck you in with grace.
I know the plans I have for you, to shape and melt you down.
Not for evil, but for good, I've worn the thorny crown.

"I am tender. I am truth. Beckon only Me.
Courage. Strength. Everlasting love. I have set you free.
Do not consider the things of old. Your future is bright and new.
Great things spring forth; I'll make the road. Trust Me in all you do.
I'll walk with you. I'll dance with you. You are worthy, you will see.
Look not back—look straight ahead. You must hold on to Me.

"Forgiveness is My gift to you. You shall point the way.
Others will see My grace in you, and they won't go astray.
You will be a light to them, a beacon on a hill.
I will lead your every step as you seek to do My will.
Arise My child. Be brave. Go forth. Your strength comes from
    above.
I'll cover you with dignity. I'll wrap you in My love."

Chapter 21

Battling Your Enemy

Fighting temptation can be exhausting. Walking a path of sexual purity in a world that is opposed to God's ideal takes fortitude and perseverance. Sometimes we do our best, we try as hard as we can, but we fail. This is what happened to Zoey.

> I tried so hard. I read this book. I committed to save the Gift. I did my best to flee temptation, but then one time, one moment of weakness, and I gave in. It's hopeless. I am such a failure. I give up.

To Zoey and to everyone else who has tried to follow God's ways but ended up "blowing it," we say, *"Don't give up!"* This is exactly what Satan *wants* you to do. It is at this moment, when you are most vulnerable, that Satan will use one of his most devious tools against you. The following illustration describes what this tool is.

> The devil decided to have a garage sale. On the day of the sale, his tools were placed for public inspection, each marked with its sales price. There were a treacherous lot of implements: hatred, envy, jealousy, deceit, lust, lying, pride, and on and on.
>
> Off on a table by itself was a harmless-looking tool. It was quite worn, but the price was VERY high.
>
> "What is the name of this tool?" asked one of the customers, pointing to it.
>
> "Discouragement." Satan replied.
>
> "Why is it priced so high?"

"Because it is more useful to me than all the other tools. I can pry open and get inside a woman's heart with Discouragement, even when I cannot get near her with the others. It is badly worn because I use it on almost everyone, since so few people know it belongs to me."[1]

Discouragement is Satan's most destructive tool. Don't let him trick you into feeling defeated. Fight back. Tell Satan that he'd better turn his ugly face in the other direction and run as fast as he can because you are coming after him with a few tools of your own—three divine spiritual weapons supplied by the living God.

Let's look at three spiritual weapons that will help you deflect Satan's darts of discouragement and defeat his evil schemes: Spiritual caller ID, the sword of the Word, and the banner of praise.

Weapon 1: Spiritual Caller ID

Second Corinthians 10 says: "We use God's mighty weapons, not mere worldly weapons, to knock down the Devil's strongholds. We…take captive every thought to make it obedient to Christ" (verse 4, NLT; verse 5, NIV).

Do you see what these verses are saying? Do you catch the truth? Our thoughts can be used as a weapon against Satan. Generally speaking, our thoughts come from three sources:

1. God
2. Satan
3. Self

"God-thoughts" are always true. The ultimate purpose of a God-thought is to glorify God by conforming us to the image of Christ. "Satan-thoughts" are lies. The ultimate goal of a Satan-thought is to thwart God's purposes and destroy those who serve Him. "Self-thoughts" are personal desires or observations. Since our focus in this section is the spiritual battle, we will concentrate on thoughts from Satan and God as they relate to sexuality.

Imagine that a thought pops into your head and you wonder, *Where did* that *thought come from?* Wouldn't it be helpful if you could identify if it was from Satan (so you could demolish it) or from God (so you could take it captive)?

There is a way. It's called "spiritual caller ID."

Do you have caller ID on your telephone? We love our caller ID—we think it is the best invention since styling gel. You know how it works. The phone rings, and you look at the screen on your caller ID so you can decide what to do with the call. If the screen shows the name of a friend you are anxious to talk with, you grab the phone, but if it shows the name of an annoying guy who has been bugging you for a date, you may choose to ignore the call.

Your spiritual caller ID works the same way. When a thought comes into your mind, you can determine the source of your thought by pausing it on the screen of your mind and asking yourself two questions:

> *Is this thought true?*
> *Does this thought please God?*

If the answer to both questions is no, this thought is most likely from Satan. If the answer is yes, the thought is most likely from God. For example, let's say you and your boyfriend begin exploring each other's bodies, and this thought enters your mind: *We're going to get married anyway. Surely God will understand if we don't wait…*

Ask yourself, *Is this thought true? Does it please God?* Because the answer to both questions is no, you can assume that this thought is from Satan. Remember, his goal is to kill, steal, and destroy, and for you to embrace this thought would certainly line up with Satan's goals!

What do you do with this thought? Hang up, NOW! But beware! Satan is not only annoying; he is persistent. If he rings again with this cheap line, ignore him and redirect your energies. Eventually he'll give up and go away.

Now suppose this thought pops into your mind: *It's important to wait... I want my wedding night to be special.*

Is this thought true? Does it please God? The answer to both questions is a resounding yes. So this thought is obviously from God.

Let's try one more. Let's say this thought comes to mind: *Touching him where he wants to be touched is okay—just as long as he keeps his clothes on.*

Again ask yourself the two questions.

Is the thought true? No! Three times the Song of Solomon warns: "Do not stir up nor awaken love until it pleases" (2:7; 3:5; 8:4, NKJV). In the Old Testament, God established a law that said that if a woman touched a man's genitals (other than her husband's), her hand was to be cut off (Deuteronomy 25:11-12). It's a good thing we are not under the Levitical law today, or we'd see lots of women with bandaged hands!

Does this thought please God? Absolutely not! Therefore, we can assume that this thought is from the Enemy, and you should immediately "hang up" on this thought.

Spiritual caller ID enables you to "source" your thoughts, making it an invaluable weapon against the Enemy. The two questions—true? and pleasing?—will help you to quickly determine what to do with a thought —hang up or hang on.

At first, sourcing these messages takes time, but with practice you will soon process your thoughts with lightning speed. You have friends whose voices are so familiar that all they have to say is "hi," and you immediately know who it is. Eventually you will develop this same ability to discern between God's voice and Satan's voice. Their voices are distinct; their purposes are vastly different.

Here is the way one young woman describes how she distinguishes between God's voice and Satan's voice.

God's voice is comforting yet convicting——but waaaaay quiet. He often speaks in a gentle whisper that forces me to listen intently. Although He makes strong recommendations, He never demands. On the other hand, Satan's voice is insistent, urging, and, well, oily. His voice is smooth evil embedded in persuasive logic. He is demanding in a "how could you possibly think otherwise?" sort of way.

Your spiritual caller ID is a powerful weapon in your battle for purity. Another weapon is the sword of the Word.

Weapon 2: The Sword of God's Word

Use every piece of God's armor to resist the enemy in the time of evil, so that after the battle you will still be standing firm.... Take the sword of the Spirit, which is the word of God. (Ephesians 6:13,17, NLT)

In Ephesians 6:13-17, we see that God provides a spiritual armor for us to wear as we battle our enemy. Each piece is designed for our protection *except* one. This weapon is the gleaming, shining sword of God's Word, and its double-edged blade cuts at the heart of Satan's evil intention and exposes his lies (Hebrews 4:12).

Jesus shows us how to use this sword against the tempter. During His lifetime, He battled against every imaginable temptation, including sexual sin.[2]

On one occasion Jesus was led into the wilderness for forty days to undergo an intense time of testing. When He was hungry, Satan challenged Him to turn stones into bread. Jesus swiped at the tempter with the sword: "*It is written,* 'Man shall not live on bread alone, but on every word that proceeds out of the mouth of God'" (Matthew 4:4, emphasis added).

Again Satan tempted Jesus, and again He thrust the sword: "*It is also written:* 'Do not put the Lord your God to the test' " (Matthew 4:7, NIV, emphasis added).

After forty days of this, Satan was frustrated. Would Jesus never abandon His unwavering loyalty to the Almighty? He pulled out the most enticing gem in his bag of tricks as he showed Jesus all the kingdoms of the world and their splendor. "All this I will give you...if you will bow down and worship me." Jesus jabbed, "Away from me, Satan! *For it is written:* 'Worship the Lord your God, and serve him only' " (Matthew 4:9-10, NIV, emphasis added).

Defeated, the devil withdrew.

Lucifer is ruthless and persistent; when one ploy fails, he tries another,

After Julie confessed the sin of her abortion, Satan continued to assault her with feelings of guilt. She discovered three ways to combat Satan's attacks by wielding the sword of the Word.

1.   Read aloud Psalm 32:5: "I acknowledged my sin to You, and my iniquity I did not hide; I said, 'I will confess my transgressions to the LORD'; and You forgave the guilt of my sin."

2.   God revealed to me that when I confessed the sin of my abortion, He took that sin and threw it as far as the east is from the west and remembers it no more. He told me that He now owns that sin and He has chosen to forget it. So when Satan reminds me that in 1979 I took my child's life, I now tell him that I don't own that sin anymore and he needs to take it up with the Owner!

3.   If Satan continues to remind me of my past, then I remind him of his future!

but the Word of God is a powerful, effective weapon against the Enemy. Faithful use of it will cause Satan to retreat in defeat.

How can you use the sword when you are faced with sexual temptation? Like Jesus, either quote or paraphrase Scripture and speak it to the Enemy.

If Satan places this thought in your mind, *There is nothing wrong with imagining how it would feel to have my boyfriend's hands all over my body,* pull out the sword and poke him with Philippians 4:8. Say, "No, Satan. I refuse to dwell on wrong thoughts and choose instead to dwell on what is PURE, RIGHT, and HONORABLE."

If the Enemy comes stalking with this thought, *I don't need sexual boundaries. There is nothing wrong with being alone in his apartment late at night,* stab him with 2 Timothy 2:22: "No. I will flee youthful lusts."

When friends invite you to an R-rated movie that you know contains explicit sex scenes, and Satan urges, *Go ahead and join them. You are an adult—what's the harm?* brandish Psalm 101:3 (NIV): "I will set before my eyes no vile thing."

The sword is a strong weapon in our battle for sexual purity, but it can only be used if we have it in hand! What scriptures do you have memorized that will help you when you are tempted? We cannot overstate the importance of knowing and using God's Word. God does not want us to retreat but to advance in the realm of the spirit by using this sword in the mighty way He intended.

Weapon 3: The Banner of Praise

> I will praise you, O LORD, with all my heart; I will tell of all your wonders. I will be glad and rejoice in you; I will sing praise to your name, O Most High. (Psalm 9:1-2, NIV)

There are times when life is hard and we just don't feel like praising God, but in this verse David introduces us to the concept of a sacrifice of praise. Four different times David says "I will" praise God. King David knew the value of releasing praise from his lips because, as he says in Psalm 22:3, God inhabits the praises of His people.

God manifests Himself through our praise. We lift Him up, and He becomes like a banner over us. Moses built an altar to God and called it *Yahweh Nissi,* which means, "The LORD is my Banner" (Exodus 17:15, NIV). In Moses' day banners were important symbols of unity and strength of purpose.[3] Moses saw God as a flag that flew over the Israelites and signaled to their enemies that the army came not in their own strength but in the power of the Most High God.

When we raise the banner of praise, we signal to our enemy that we come NOT in our power but in the power of God. The flag expresses our allegiance to the King. Our enemy is aware that the King is over us, and we are under the King's protection.

How do you raise the banner of praise? Perhaps as you've read this book, the accuser has assaulted you with thoughts like these:

I'll never get married.

I'll never have sex.

I'll always be alone.

When this happens, raise the banner of praise by saying:

> *I praise You, God, that You have great plans for me*
> *whether I get married or not. I thank You, Lord,*
> *that I am never alone, because You are always with me.*

When Satan sees the banner of praise, his hands tremble and his knees buckle. Doing battle with you is no big deal, but the fact that you are under the banner of praise means you are part of God's army, and Satan fights not just you but the Lord of Hosts. That's an entirely different matter!

We are weak. We have no strength. We cannot succeed when we face the Enemy alone. But when we pick up the banner of praise, our enemy runs and our own spirits are encouraged.

Won't you raise the banner now?

O Great God of Truth, I praise You.
You are Lord over all, Ruler of all creation.
I shout for joy to my Lord and King.
Lord, teach me to take my thoughts captive.
Show me how to use the sword of Your Word.
May I lift high the banner of praise.
Be glorified in my life, O Holy God.

Praise the Lord.

~

Waiting for the Gift

Come, My daughter.
    Let Me encourage your heart.
    I know the wait is lonely.
        I know the wait seems long.
I understand the ache. I desire to soothe the
      longing.
Let My words bring you comfort.
    Let My words fill you with hope.

Come.
Refresh yourself in Me
    as you wait.

Chapter 22

The Long, Lonely Wait

Waiting is agony. You long to share your life with someone, to connect in deep oneness—thought to thought, heart to heart, and spirit to spirit. You yearn for a soul mate who will listen to you, someone with whom you can share your hopes and dreams. As you've read this book you've become increasingly eager to put into practice what you have learned about the Gift. Between each line of text the unspoken question lingers: How long must I wait?

Waiting. It's not a pleasant subject, is it?

The mantra of the twenty-first century is: NOW! We want what we want when we want it. Our culture has conditioned us to receive immediate gratification. As a result, waiting is an unwelcome intrusion that produces within us finger-drumming, stomach-churning, brow-creasing frustration.

You know well the frustration of waiting. Your insides churn with each tick, tick, tick of your biological clock. Every friend's wedding or baby shower sets off an ear-piercing alarm. Like an icicle on a warm day, your happiness melts, leaving you in a puddle of tears. You tell yourself:

"I'll never be a bride."

"The other side of my bed will always be empty."

"I'll never have kids."

Or, for the more pragmatic:

"I'm forever destined to mow my own yard."

The following entry from a friend's journal expresses this silent ache.

Dear One,

It's a Friday evening, and my plane has been delayed. I'm returning to Nashville for business. I'm wondering if we are going to meet on this trip. I don't really know, but it is fun just to imagine a "maybe." A small part of me is hoping and expecting that perhaps this trip, this time, we may meet.

I miss you. I miss you here, in these quiet moments, among the activity of the usual and routine. How can it be that I both need you and don't need you; that I long for your presence yet find myself complete without you; that I hope to have my world vastly opened by your being made real, yet find it already so intriguing and inexhaustible?

Perhaps when we first meet, I will feel right away that I am being given a gift—the gift of love that exists between a man and a woman. I hope I recognize you—not in a "love at first sight" kind of way—but something deeper, something more real. I want your heart to first belong to the Lord. He's teaching me the same. I am praying for you. I've already begun loving you…is that possible?

Love, Me

This young woman hopes that God will soon bring that special someone into her life. Her hope will likely be realized, but she has no guarantee. Some women wait many years before they marry; others never marry at all. The wait can be difficult and filled with uncertainty. Keep reading, and glean wisdom from two single women as they share their thoughts about the waiting game.

Patti Ann

I blew out the candles on yet another birthday cake last week. It wasn't my twenty-fifth, or even my thirty-fifth for that matter. In many ways, my life has surpassed the hopes I had as a twelve-year-old who went to slumber parties and dreamed with my girlfriends about what we wanted to do when we grew up and who we would marry. Some things have turned out like I dreamed, but my life is far from what I would have chosen. You see, I've never been married—and I'm a virgin.

I've dated many men, and I've had just about as much heartbreak, but I don't have many regrets. I've done some stupid things, but I am grateful to God that I don't have to ignore an old boyfriend across the room at a Christmas party or in the grocery store. I'm glad I can look him in the eye, smile, and wish him well and that I don't have to deal with a heart full of anger or bitterness over what I allowed him to take from me.

The path of purity is difficult. When I'm sitting in a church pew, listening to a rousing sermon about the evils of sex outside of marriage and how it is best to save myself for my soul mate, my spirit cries "yes!" When I'm curled up on the sofa, sipping a cup of hot chocolate, and reading about how God can fulfill me and satisfy my deepest needs, I nod in agreement. But it's a whole different story when I'm alone with the man of my dreams and I think that he loves me just as much as I love him. When the hormones are surging, I'm amazed at how quickly my perspective can change about what is right and…well…what might not be so wrong.

I've had my share of words with my heavenly Father about the whole issue of sex. I've cried. I've sulked. I've bargained. At times, I've whined like a child, turning my back and crossing my arms as I pouted in the corner. His answer has never changed, but I know deep down that my only reasonable option is to obey. I know that God's way is always best for me. As I trust in Him for the will and strength to obey in this area, I feel joy and peace—a buoyant hope that shines beyond the loneliness and longing.

I've had mixed feelings as I've watched the years go by, but one of the blessings of age is perspective, a larger view of life, and a chance to watch the test of time. I've seen the "rest of the story" in some areas of my life and the lives of friends. I've seen their choices played out; the tolls they have taken or the blessings they have brought. It's hard to wait for sex until marriage, but through the years, I've seen that life is harder, and the price is greater, for those who do not wait.

Jill

For me, the hardest thing about waiting is being *reminded* that I am waiting. Like when I'm picking out a movie on Saturday night, and everyone else at Blockbuster is part of a couple. Or when my car develops a new noise, and I don't know how to fix it or where to take it, or when I'm sick and have no one to run to the store to pick up some medicine for me.

Still, I reject the notion that because I am single my life is on hold. I don't feel that my life is incomplete without a husband. While I dearly want a husband and see ways God has been culti-vating my heart in this direction, I know that in Christ alone, I am complete.

A friend who is ten years older than me recently confessed that she feels that God has forgotten her. She knows in her head that He has not, but the circumstances in her life—she's single and childless and has to support herself—add up to a different life than she thought she would be living at her age.

I can relate because my life is very different than what my soul wants it to be. I can be gripped by the fear that I might still be single when I reach her age. But I don't want to be controlled by fear, so what do I do?

I go back to something bigger than myself—I go to God and His Word. In God's Word I find promises. His promises are real to me because God is trustworthy. What I read isn't just theology; it is Truth, Truth that speaks to the questions my heart and mind ask.

This Truth is often a paradox. Some days are so discouraging and seemingly without purpose. Other days, I feel strong and capable, bursting with an irrepressible hope. Because I go back and forth, I need an anchor—I want an anchor. Jesus is my anchor. He centers me. He reminds me who I am and where my home is.

My relationship with Jesus contains endless mysteries and paths of learning. This is precious and real to me. I have learned in small measure what it means for Jesus to be my husband, my lover, my intimate, my confidant. I know and believe that during the times of stress or displeasure, my Lord is etching into my soul and building into my character the things that will bring Him glory.

The bottom line is this: God is bigger than anything I am going through, and He wants something bigger for my life than I want for myself. God can be trusted.

EVERYONE HAS TO WAIT

Like Jill and Patti Ann, the psalmist found himself in waiting mode. We hear his lament in the following words:

I am shriveled like a wineskin in the smoke, exhausted with waiting. But I cling to your principles and obey them. How long must I wait? (Psalm 119:83-84, NLT)

None of us like to wait, yet we all find ourselves in a waiting mode at some point in our lives. Some women wait to have a baby, others wait to see their husbands come to Christ, still others wait for their child to be healed or their marriage to be more intimate. Single women can fall into the trap of thinking they are the only ones who have to wait, but this isn't true. Everyone waits...some wait for months, others for years. Waiting is a part of life, married or single.

The ways of God are a mystery, and often there are no satisfying answers to the whys of waiting. Still, waiting is never without purpose, and as we wait, God desires to work in our lives. If we let Him, God will

- strengthen our character (Romans 5:3-5)
- teach us about His character (Isaiah 64:4)
- show us something that can help someone else (2 Corinthians 1:3-4)

If this is true, and if we trust that waiting is part of God's sovereign plan for the prescribed moment, the question suddenly changes. We no longer ask *should* I wait, but *how* should I wait.

HOW SHALL WE THEN WAIT?

There are two types of "waiters"—*passive* and *active*.

A *passive* waiter lives in standby mode, putting her life on hold until she gets married. She thinks, *When I get married, I'll do this.* Or, *When I have a husband, I will be that.* Her only action is to occasionally check her watch, wondering why Mr. Right is so late.

In her loneliness, the passive waiter becomes indiscriminant about the company she keeps. She lounges on the couch of her singleness, and before she can fluff her pillow, the Destructive D's of Discontent, Discouragement, Despair, and Depression nestle in beside her. They smother her as they scoot over to make room for their nasty cousins, the A's—Anxiety and Anger. These companions so monopolize her time and space that her life has no room for God or for giving to others.

What a contrast to the *active* waiter. The active waiter finds purpose in every moment. She eagerly grabs hold of life and squeezes adventure and possibility out of each situation. Through the waiting, she develops an enviable trust in God. Psalm 37:3-7 (NIV) describes the active waiter:

Trust in the LORD and do good [by reaching out to others];

Dwell in the land [make your home, settle down, be at peace where God puts you].

Delight yourself in the LORD [make the Lord your only joy], and he will give you the desires of your heart.

Commit your life [totally and unreservedly] to the LORD;
Trust in him and he will do this:…
Be still before the LORD and
Wait patiently for him.[1]

Trust, dwell, delight, commit, be still, and wait are all imperatives—they are not suggestions but commands. But of all the commands in Psalm 37, "wait patiently" is the most difficult. We can do this only if we have knelt at the altar of God's timetable with open hands and an open heart and prayed:

> But as for me, I trust in You, O LORD; I say, "You are my God."
> My times are in Your hand. (Psalm 31:14-15, NKJV)

Waiting is an offering and a sacrifice. We may lift up our very waiting to God, in a spirit of expectancy, asking only for His agenda. As Elisabeth Elliot observed, "Waiting on God in this way is true faith—no agenda of one's own, no deadlines, no demands on what God must do. Simply an open heart and open hands ready to receive that which God shall choose, and a perfect confidence that what He chooses will be better than our best."[2]

And joy of joys—as we wait, bowing to God's plan and purposes for our life, He promises to meet us in the agony of waiting.

What does He promise?

- *To hear you.* "I waited patiently for the LORD; and He inclined to me and heard my cry.… He put a new song in my mouth, a song of praise to our God" (Psalm 40:1,3).
- *To work for you.* "From ages past no one has heard, no ear has perceived, no eye has seen any God besides you, who works for those who wait for him" (Isaiah 64:4, NRSV).
- *To renew your strength.* "Those who wait for the LORD will gain new strength; they will mount up with wings like eagles, they will run and not get tired, they will walk and not become weary" (Isaiah 40:31).
- *To give you peace.* "Do not be anxious about anything, but in

everything, by prayer and petition, with thanksgiving, present your requests to God. And the peace of God, which transcends all understanding, will guard your hearts and your minds in Christ Jesus" (Philippians 4:6-7, NIV).

We can imagine our loving heavenly Father saying to you:

> *My dear daughter, do not be anxious about anything.*
> *All things are in My control.*
> *Talk to Me about your concerns.*
> *Do not look at the things that others have*
> *or what I have given them.*
> *Do not look at the things you think you want.*
> *Instead, look to Me.*
> *As you set your heart and your desires upon Me,*
> *I will give you peace. I will satisfy your longings.*
> *In Me you will find what you have been seeking.*

The following anonymous poem beautifully captures the essence of waiting on God and the satisfaction that comes from knowing Him. Read it out loud. As you do, ask God to speak to you.

Waiting

Desperately, helplessly, longingly, I cried.
Quietly, patiently, lovingly, God replied.
I pled and I wept for a clue to my fate,
The Master gently said, "Child, you must wait!"
"Wait? You say, wait!" my indignant reply.
"Lord, I need answers, I need to know why!
Is your hand shortened? Or have you not heard?
By FAITH I have asked and am claiming your Word.

"My future and all to which I can relate
Hangs in the balance, and you tell me to WAIT?

I'm needing a 'yes,' a go-ahead sign,
Or even a 'no' to which I can resign.

"And, Lord, you promised that if we believe
We need but to ask, and we shall receive.
Lord, I've been asking and this is my cry:
I'm weary of asking! I need a reply!"
Then quietly, softly, I learned of my fate.
Once again my Master replied, "You must wait."
So I slumped in my chair, defeated and taut,
And grumbled to God, "So, I'm waiting...for what?"
He seemed then to kneel, and His eyes wept with mine,
And he tenderly said, "I could give you a sign.
I could shake the heavens and darken the sun.
I could raise the dead and cause mountains to run.
All you seek I could give, and pleased you would be.
You would have what you want—but you wouldn't know ME.

"You'd not know the depth of my love for each saint;
You'd not know the power that I give to the faint;
You'd not learn to see through the clouds of despair;
You'd not learn to trust just by knowing I'm there;
You'd not know the joy of resting in me
When darkness and silence were all you could see.

"You'd never experience that fullness of love
As the peace of my Spirit descends like a dove;
You'd know that I give and I save...(for a start),
But you'd not know the depth of the beat of my heart.

"The glow of my comfort late into the night.
The faith that I give when you walk without sight,
The depth that's beyond getting just what you asked
Of an infinite God, who makes what you have LAST.

"You'd never know, should your pain quickly flee,
What it means that 'My grace is sufficient for thee.'
Yes, your dreams for your loved ones overnight would come true,
But, oh, the loss! if I lost what I'm doing in you!

"So be silent, my child, and in time you will see
THAT THE GREATEST OF GIFTS IS TO GET TO KNOW
　　　ME.
And though oft may my answers seem terribly late,
　　My wisest of answers is still but to WAIT."

Chapter 23

Nancy: One Woman's Insight

Earlier you met our friend Nancy Barton, the director of a women's ministry program who wrote out her vision statement in chapter 13. You might remember that she said that if she had known that she would still be single at forty-four, she would have said to the Lord, "Stop this planet. I want off!" Yet Nancy has persisted on the path of purity, and her faithfulness in waiting has reaped rich insights that we believe will encourage and help you. We interviewed Nancy and asked if we could share our conversation with you. She graciously agreed.

Q: Waiting can be agonizing. What do you say to single women who are faced with the reality that God's timetable is NOT their timetable?

A: As singles, we can feel that God has forgotten us. We try to speed up God's timetable by dating just to date, often settling for less than God's best because we feel desperate. We do a "silent fistfight" with God and dwell on what we *don't* have rather than on what we *do* have. Consequently, we miss out on the joys of surrender. We miss out on days filled with contentment, peace, and joy simply because we fight against God's timetable.

Over the years I have come to trust in God's sovereignty. I have seen the perfection of His timetable in so many other areas of my life that I can trust that He is on time in this area too.

God is active in the waiting—He often uses this time to fashion within us our greatest character qualities. I am a much different woman today than I was at twenty-five. God has strengthened my character through the crucible of waiting.

Q: How do you handle the pain that comes with waiting?

A: I think different women handle it in different ways. However, it's important to do the right thing with our pain. I see so many singles unwilling to walk through the doorway of pain and suffering. One woman I know has turned to exercise and competitive activities in order to "kill" her pain. I know others who keep themselves extremely busy just to avoid a night at home in a quiet house. Some women consume themselves in their work or in ministry.

I think we run to other things because we secretly doubt God—He can't possibly be big enough to embrace the pain we feel! And so we withhold our pain from Him and fill the holes instead with temporary painkillers. By faith, we must step into the pain, not fear it, realizing that Jesus will catch us. Once we've experienced His catch, we're hungry for more of Him; temporary painkillers have less appeal.

I've always had lots of close friends, and I found it easier to call upon a friend than to call upon God when I was in pain. God moved me several times to different locations, and I could no longer count on friends to subside the pain of singleness. I came to realize that only God would always be there to listen and comfort me.

I have to put one foot in front of the other, obeying God even when I don't feel very strong. When singleness seems unbearable, I often kneel at my bedside and gaze at a drawing of Jesus holding a woman crying in His arms. It is a vivid reminder that Jesus is my burden bearer and longs to ease my pain. I truly worship as I weep!

Q: Being single in a couple's world must be very challenging.

A: It is! Last year I was a part of a small-group discussion where six out of the nine women at our table were pregnant. Sitting at that table was a glaring reminder of my constant, unfulfilled desire to have a husband and children. After one study I cried with some married friends and spoke about my struggle. I left that day encouraged and lifted up in prayer.

As singles we are sometimes too proud to let others know how deeply hard singleness really is. We have forgotten that the carrying of a cross is not a private act, but a very public act. In *The Gospel According to Job,* Mike Mason says that we are so caught up in projecting to others an outer image that is better than what's really going on inside. Instead of glorying in our weaknesses as Paul did, we hide them.[1] As singles we must run to Jesus with our pain, and when He directs, we must openly share our weaknesses with others.

We sometimes complain that married people don't really know how tough it is as a single, but how can they know unless we tell them? We do ourselves and others a disservice by hiding the hurts of our heart, because we rob others of the joy of ministering to us.

Q: Are there certain situations that are more painful than others?

A: Holidays in general are hard. When I was younger, I could spend holidays with single friends, but as I've gotten older, most of my friends are married with families of their own. Valentine Day can be particularly painful for me because I oversee Valentine Day events at our church. I have a responsibility before God to lead the planning meetings with enthusiasm and excitement. I have to intentionally focus on welcoming Jesus as my partner at these events.

Weddings and baby showers can also be challenging. It's been hard to "rejoice with those who rejoice" when my cries for these things go unanswered. I've been jealous of friends who suddenly announced that they were engaged. But then I read Amy Carmichael's words—"See in this a chance to die"—and realized that I could view engagements, weddings, and baby showers as opportunities to die to self-centeredness, self-pity, and comparison. This perspective has helped me to write congratulations cards, purchase gifts, look for ways to assist in wedding plans, and pray for my engaged friends. God has taken my self-pity and turned it into joy.

I can't do this without God's help. I talk to Jesus when I have to attend an event that may bring up feelings of loneliness and self-pity. I tell Him how hard it is to always bless others who have what I want. I ask Him for supernatural love and strength to do what I can't do on my own. I then go with a mission and ask the Holy Spirit, "I wonder whom I can bless tonight?" As we bless others, we will be blessed. I thank God for the many couples I've influenced as I set aside self-pity and sought the greater good!

Q: We have talked about the difference between active waiting and passive waiting. Describe how this looks in your life.

A: Active waiting is intentional and purposeful, similar to the way we approach our spiritual growth. If I truly want to become conformed to the image of Christ, I must commit to certain actions. I must partner with the Holy Spirit, practice spiritual disciplines, and welcome as friends the trials God brings my way. This is based on the Golden Triangle of Spiritual Formation, from Dallas Willard's book *The Divine Conspiracy.*

Q: Hold on. That sounds like good stuff. Tell us more about these three points and how they apply to your singleness.

A: *Partnering with the Holy Spirit* appears at the apex of the triangle, which displays its importance in the transformation process. As we grow spiritually, the Spirit works in and through us to practice and live in Christlikeness. I partner with the Holy Spirit in living my singleness as Jesus would. Every day becomes a day of intending to live like Jesus. In addition, the Spirit enables me to grow the kind of inward character that displays itself in my outward life: love, joy, peace, patience, kindness, goodness, faithfulness, gentleness, and self-control (Galatians 5:22-23).

The second point of the triangle involves *practicing spiritual disciplines.* Spiritual disciplines enable us to turn from depending on our human ability and to depend on God. I use spiritual disciplines to lay aside wrong habits and gain new habits that enable me to be more Christlike, including memorizing Scripture, practicing solitude, meditating, praying, fasting, and worshiping. When I struggle with busyness, I might take a "soul care" day with God. If I'm struggling with self-pity, I might pray regularly for joy and contentment.

The last point of the triangle is to *welcome as friends the trials God brings my way*. We can make James 1:2-4 a practical reality of life. Instead of avoiding trials, we can see every event and challenge as an opportunity for God to work. For example, instead of avoiding a lonely weekend because it might be painful, I can welcome it, knowing that God can use it to mature my character. We often miss the positive side of trials simply because we don't welcome them as friends!

Q: Many single women write in journals to their future husbands and pray for them. Do you think this is wise, or does it build false hope?

A: I pray regularly for my future husband. I pray for his purity, his character, his vocation. I don't see this as raising false hope. Instead, it is a way I can build into his life and bless him, even though I don't know him.

I think that we, as singles, need to recognize the power of shameless asking. God wants us to persistently express the desires of our hearts. I've known single women who have given up praying for a husband. We sometimes stop praying for something simply because we get tired of asking and not receiving. We wonder if God hears us. But I'm convinced we must ask and ask for God's best and never stop!

John 16:24 says, "Until now you have asked for nothing in My name; ask and you will receive, so that your joy may be made full." We must ask with open, submissive hands, wanting only what God wants. Luke 11:5-13 talks about how God the Father loves to give good gifts to His children. God wants our best. But if what we ask for will hurt us, He will not give it. I want to accept God's will but not to be passive. I am convinced that, as a single, God wants me to continue to be expectant and to stay in a posture of asking.

Q: Okay, get practical. Describe how active waiting looks when it comes to men.

A: This may sound odd, but I study the opposite sex. I actively build friendships with men and find ways to interact with single men on a regular basis. I try to keep an open mind when it comes to singles groups, community activities, blind dates, or other places where I can meet godly Christian men.

I must admit this wasn't always the case. I have had a cynical spirit about singles events or attending things where I might meet single Christian men. Just last year, while on a missions trip, God revealed to me how my cynical spirit had prevented me from starting an older singles ministry at our church. I was overwhelmed with grief. I have since started a new thirty-five-plus ministry for our church and community. Often, because of a bad experience or wounded heart, single women retreat from men and fail to take advantage of opportunities that could have been a blessing to them. May God break through our pride!

Q: Nancy, you've shared many rich insights. We appreciate your honesty and transparency. We have one last question. This one may be the toughest of all. What do you do with your sexual urges?

A: What a loaded question! Well, I certainly have them, and they have grown stronger as I've gotten older. Just the other night I was reading a Christian book on sexuality and singles. Sprinkled throughout the book were personal stories about sexuality. I found myself sexually excited just reading them! As I finished skimming the book, I realized the only place to go was to my knees. I knelt beside my bed and begged God to satisfy my soul with His love. I slept soundly and peacefully that night.

I try to exercise regularly. So much of managing sexual urges has to do with controlling our bodies. I also have a close friend and counselor who knows my "stuff"; she knows my struggles and areas of weakness. She holds me accountable in this area, and that accountability has been a source of strength and practical help for corralling my sexual urges.

I also have a dog! Seriously, it helps to have an outlet for my affections. Gracie Lou gets lots of hugs and kisses. But what helps most is to stay close to Jesus and allow Him to be the lover and satisfier of my soul. This is everything…EVERYTHING!

The Higher Gift

Come, beloved.
A Higher Gift awaits you.
Now is the moment to unveil the mystery.
Now is the time to reveal hidden
truth.
I show you the Higher Gift because I love
you.
Lift your eyes.
Open your ears.
Quiet your heart.
What once was secret, I now make known
to you.

Chapter 24

A Life~Changing Secret

Madeline studied her reflection in the mirror with wide-eyed wonder. The rumpled white chiffon dress she had pulled out of her dress-up box was many sizes too big. A white towel secured by bobby pins trailed down her back, a bulky bridal veil. Dusty plastic daisies served as her bridal bouquet. A broad smile lit her face. She looked so pretty.

Clomp, clomp, clomp. She turned and plodded down the hall toward the kitchen in her oversized pumps to show off her make-believe wedding ensemble. "Mommy, Mommy, look at me! One day I'm going to be a real bride."

Twenty Years Later

Madeline wiggled her toes in the white satin pumps, wishing she'd bought a larger size. Her feet hurt, but she couldn't think about that now. In a moment she would walk down the aisle.

The church was packed with people she had known for years. Flowers and candles adorned the sanctuary. The pianist was about to play the music that would call her forward.

A voice beside her whispered, "Always a bridesmaid, never a bride, huh, Madeline? But your turn will come, I know it will."

The words were meant to encourage, but she could not deny the sting. Her flowered organdy dress was a sharp contrast beside the white flowing gown that graced her friend.

Then another Voice whispered, One she alone heard. "Remember the Higher Gift, beloved. Remember the secret we share…"

In this book you've learned some life-changing truths. You have seen that

- You are a Gift and have been gift-wrapped by God.
- You *can* become as a virgin again.
- Your vision statement is a powerful tool to help you save the Gift.
- You *can* guard the Gift from your enemy.
- You *can* wait actively.

And now we want to tell you another truth. If you fully embrace this truth, it can forever change how you view yourself as a single woman and revolutionize your view of God. Are you ready?

You are a bride!

You are a bride—*now!* Does this change how you view yourself? It should! Go ahead and read the words again. This is a LIFE-CHANGING truth. Pray over this revelation, and soak in its meaning. *Selah.*[1]

But wait, there's more. You are not just *any* bride; you are the radiant, glowing bride of the King of kings and the Lord of lords. You are the bride of Christ. This is a paradox. Although Scripture says that you become "married" to the bridegroom at the heavenly marriage feast of the Lamb, Jesus calls you His bride NOW.

Felicia, age twenty-one, called us after reading this chapter and said excitedly, "Thank you! Thank you for showing me that I am a bride *now*. I'd heard all the reasons for waiting to have sex, but I needed more than a set of rules. I needed a greater vision, a higher purpose. Before I knew that I was *supposed* to wait; now I understand *why* I should wait—because I am the bride of Christ."

GOD'S HEART FOR YOU

Although you may have heard before that you are the bride of Christ, you likely have never fully understood your identity in this role—and when you do understand, you will see that your daily choices for purity have eternal significance. Images of the bride of Christ are woven throughout Scripture. As we set out the biblical framework for this imagery, it gets a little "heady," but stay with us! You will see how all of this applies to you personally. So come back, back to the beginning to see what was in the heart of God before Creation.

From Genesis to Revelation we see that God had a divine purpose in mind: to procure for Himself an eternal companion. All of history will one day culminate in one glorious event, one grand celebration—the wedding of God's Son at the marriage feast of the Lamb (Revelation 19:8-9).

Who is the bride that Christ will marry? Scripture makes it abundantly clear that the bride of Christ is the church—every believer, and that includes YOU. You are an individual, but you are also a member of a corporate body, and this body will one day become the bride of Christ (1 Corinthians 12:14-25). The bride will include people from every nation and tongue, but amazingly Jesus relates to each of us in such a personal way that we feel we are the sole object of His eternal affection.

God's Word clearly pictures Christ calling, wooing, and winning His bride. Scripture outlines three steps in this process. First, Jesus expresses His love for His bride (John 15:12). Next, Christ promises to take His bride to the Father's house (John 14:2-3; 1 Thessalonians 4:13-18). Finally, Scripture describes the marriage supper, or wedding feast, when the marriage will be consummated (Revelation 19:7-9). The last two events will happen in the future. But in the present, the glorious truth is this: *If you have accepted Christ's offer of salvation, you are His betrothed.*

THE COURTSHIP

Today when a young man wants to marry a young woman, he will ask her to be his wife, perhaps seek her father's blessing, and then slip a ring on her finger. In Jesus' time this process was a bit more complicated. In addition to asking the father's blessing, the prospective groom also had to negotiate a *mohar* with the bride's father. The *mohar* is the price he would pay for the honor of marrying the bride.

Once the price was established, the couple would drink from a cup of wine, an act that symbolized the sealing of their marriage covenant. A blessing was pronounced, and from that moment forward the bride was regarded as the wife of the bridegroom.[2] This engagement was so binding that unfaithfulness required a certificate of divorce. A wife in spirit now, she would become a wife in practice when the marriage was consummated on the wedding day.

Jesus followed the wedding customs of the day. He came as a bridegroom, boldly declaring His love for you, the bride (Matthew 9:15). He negotiated the *mohar* with your Father. The price was staggering. If Jesus wanted you as His bride, He would have to prove His love by dying for you. No other groom would consider such an outlandish request, but Jesus was no ordinary groom, nor is His love for you an ordinary love.

On the night before His death, Jesus held up the cup of wine during the Last Supper and said, "This is My blood of the covenant, which is poured out for many. Truly I say to you, I will never again drink of the fruit of the vine until that day when I drink it new in the kingdom of God" (Mark 14:24-25). Then He drank from the cup and offered it to His bride, represented by the disciples, who also drank, sealing the betrothal. The following day Jesus surrendered His life. The *mohar* was paid in full (Mark 10:45).

If you have accepted Christ's proposal, you are not your own. You have been bought with a price (1 Corinthians 6:20). You are betrothed to Christ. One day at the glorious marriage feast of the Lamb, you will consummate your union with your bridegroom. Until that day you are engaged to Jesus (spiritually speaking). And just as was true of engaged couples in Jesus' time, as your groom He regards you *now* as His wife. This is how we can say that you are the bride of Christ—*now*.

We love God's Word. Not only is it perfect, flawless, and profitable for instruction; it often tells two stories in one. God often uses a small story to communicate a larger story, an earthly image to convey a heavenly picture. One story, two messages. One image, two very different interpretations. The first image paints a physical picture; the second, a spiritual picture.

Second Corinthians 11:2 is an example of a small truth that symbolizes a larger truth:

> I promised you to one husband, to Christ, so that I might present
> you as a pure virgin to him. (NIV)

The Gift of your physical purity to your earthly husband is the small story. It is a symbol of the larger story of the Gift of your spiritually pure heart and soul that you will give to your heavenly bridegroom, Christ. We wrote this book to help you remain a virgin, but this verse tells you why this is so important.

Granted, the spiritual nature of this concept is difficult to grasp. It is one thing to give intellectual assent to the truth that you are the bride of Christ; it is another thing entirely to experience the love of Christ on a daily basis. What does it mean that Jesus is your bridegroom? How should this truth impact you on a daily basis? We will share some answers with you in the next few chapters.

Chapter 25

Jesus, Your Bridegroom

A college girl in ministry leadership makes this honest statement:

> The idea that Jesus is my bridegroom has always seemed hokey to me. After all, how can I have an intimate relationship with someone I cannot see?

What we are about to say, we say with the utmost sincerity. *We believe that the intimacy you can have with Jesus can* surpass *the intimacy you can have with any other man.* How is this possible? How can we be intimate with someone we cannot see? We learn to see in a different way—not with our physical eyes but with our spiritual eyes. Paul says:

> We fix our eyes not on what is seen, but on what is unseen.
> (2 Corinthians 4:18, NIV)

FINE-TUNING YOUR SPIRITUAL SENSES

God created us with physical senses that allow us to taste, touch, smell, hear, and see the physical world, but we also have spiritual senses that enable us to experience the unseen world. Our spiritual senses are similar to our physical senses, and they develop along the same lines.

Think for a moment about when you were born. As a baby, you could taste, touch, smell, hear, and see, but because your senses were not mature, your ability to use them to interpret the world was limited. By the time you were five years old, your senses had developed in such a way that you could process your world on a basic level. Now, as a young woman, your senses are fully developed. With this development has come certain longings, including the desire for a soul mate who will love you and share your dreams.

The formation of your spiritual senses follows a similar pattern. The moment you received Jesus as your Savior, you were "born" in spirit; your eyes were opened, and you saw Him for the first time. Because you were a baby, your spiritual senses were limited in their ability to comprehend Jesus. As you grow and mature in the Lord, your spiritual senses *quicken.* Over time, you develop greater sensitivity to Jesus, and your spirit learns to feel His touch, hear His voice, and taste His goodness (Psalm 34:8).

We've walked with Jesus many years, and He is as real to us as any human person. God has developed our spiritual senses to the point where we feel His touch in our spirits. He is our touchable, tangible Savior, our faithful Friend, and the Lover of our souls. This relationship did not happen overnight but over time—and we continue to grow in intimacy with Him.

Our love for Jesus is much greater now than when we first became Christians. Our present love is only a shadow of what our future love will be, and our future love is only a glimmer of what we will experience on that day when we see Him face to face. As 1 Corinthians 13:12 says, "Now we see but a poor reflection as in a mirror; then we shall see face to face. Now I know in part; then I shall know fully, even as I am fully known" (NIV). We can hardly wait for that day!

Dear friend, we cannot encourage you strongly enough about this. Press hard after Jesus! Turn your affections to the One who loves you, the One who longs to be intimate with you. Loving Jesus is an exciting journey, a never-ending adventure with new discoveries around each bend in the road. He is your bridegroom. He loves you passionately. He wants to be your friend, your leader, and your lover.

YOUR BRIDEGROOM IS YOUR FRIEND

First, Jesus is your friend (John 15:15). He has seen the tears you have cried over your loneliness, and He whispers, "You are not alone. I am with you" (cf. Matthew 28:20). Jesus wants you to talk to Him, to share your silliest thoughts and your deepest longings. He wants to laugh with you, to cry with you, and to walk alongside you. He wants to join you at Starbucks for coffee or go with you to a basketball game or to your friend's wedding shower. Unlike the friends in the past who have abandoned you or betrayed you, Jesus will never leave you (Deuteronomy 31:8). He believes in you. As your friend, there is nothing He won't do for you (John 15:13).

YOUR BRIDEGROOM IS YOUR LEADER

"The husband is the head of the wife" (Ephesians 5:23). Jesus is our head, our leader (1 Corinthians 11:3). Some women are thrilled at the idea of having a leader. They are tired of making all the decisions themselves, and the thought of a wise, caring leader who would direct them brings enormous relief. Other women rebel at the notion of having someone "over" them. They don't want anyone telling them what they should and should not do. But Christ is not our head so that He can be a tyrant. Jesus is a tender, compassionate servant leader. He longs to care for you, protect you, and create a nourishing environment where you can grow. Jesus is your champion, your greatest encourager. He wants you to be all that you can be, and He leads you into your potential through acts of service and sacrificial love.

YOUR BRIDEGROOM IS YOUR LOVER

Many women can relate to Jesus as friend, confidant, and companion, but they have difficulty seeing Him as a lover because of the word's sexual connotations. When we talk about Jesus as a lover, we are referring to a *spiritual* lover, not a physical lover. The purpose of His intimate love is to bring about spiritual oneness, not physical oneness.

Jesus passionately longs for spiritual oneness with you. You were created to be one with your bridegroom, to enjoy deep delight and spiritual ecstasy in your union with Him. He calls you to a divine romance, an exhilarating, intoxicating love relationship that offers joy beyond what is possible in any human relationship.

Psalm 16:11 says, "In Your presence is fullness of joy; at Your right hand are pleasures forevermore" (NKJV). *There is pleasure in knowing Jesus.* Not just nice warm feelings, but sublime joy! In fact, the pleasure that is possible in true intimacy with Jesus can be as great as any other pleasure you could imagine, including sexual pleasure.

Some women are afraid of this kind of love. It is too intense, too emotional. They can trust Jesus with their mind but not with their emotions. They fear their emotions and keep them under lock and key because being in control of their feelings makes them feel secure.

Linda: For many years I did not express deep passion directly to Jesus. I could sing, "We adore You, we long for You," but to fall on my knees and to say with every part of my being, "*I* adore You, *I* long for You," felt uncomfortable. I am a passionate person, and I could express passion to my husband and to those I loved, but somehow I couldn't do this with Jesus. My passion came out in the form of service. As a missionary, I was untiring in my work for Him. Deep within I heard Him beckon, "Come, Linda, enjoy intimacy with Me." But I responded, "Later, my Lord. I have too much to do for You."

Then God began to draw me into worship—deep, private worship. As I became free to worship with my body, the floodgates of emotion burst forth and released the passion buried in my heart. Joy unspeakable filled my being as I experienced spiritual intimacy and, yes, even ecstasy. Jesus has become the lover of my soul. Worship has become the joy of my heart.

After one beautiful time with the Lord, I wrote:

I was on my knees before the Holy One, and He took me to a place of utter silence. It was such a beautiful place that I could not move, I could not speak, I could only be. My spirit was so connected to His that it felt strange when my hand touched my face. I think I was surprised to realize that I had a body. I could not raise my hands high enough, I could not bow low enough, I could not think of words powerful enough to give honor and glory to the Holy One, the One worthy of my worship. How grateful I am that the Holy Spirit expresses my love to the Father for me.

Lorraine: One of the ways I experience Jesus as my lover is when we dance together. I love Rogers and Hammerstein's *Cinderella.* When the prince takes Cinderella into his arms, my heart swells with emotion as they swirl and spin across the dance floor as one. This image is often in my mind when I dance with Jesus. Sometimes we dance in my imagination. Other times I actually get on my feet and move with the music. If you could peek in on this intimate moment, you would see me glide and turn, my left hand clasping the hand of my unseen partner, my right arm resting on His strong shoulder. In these precious, tender times, all my longings are satisfied, everything of this earth ceases to be. There is only Jesus and me.

After one such dance I wrote in my journal:

Dear Jesus, I wish, oh, how I wish I could pause this moment and linger in it forever. I love You so much! You bless me with the joy of Your presence. Oh Lord, my heart sings to feel Your tenderness toward me. I love the companionable silence we share, the way we say nothing but speak all things.

What could be more glorious? Oh the comfort, the soul-satisfying peace I know when I nestle against Your strong frame, sink down into Your love, and move as one with You in this dance called life.

We wonder, what do you think when you read about these two crazy authors who abandon their emotions and do odd things like dance with Jesus? Please understand that we do not dance with Jesus or experience such deep emotional intimacy with Him every day—or even every week. As with any relationship, there are times of ordinariness and routine predictability. Nor are we suggesting that the way intimacy with Jesus looks for us is the way it should look for you. You are unique. Your love relationship with Jesus is like no other's. The way you experience spiritual oneness with Him will be personal to you.

Does having an intimate relationship with Jesus mean you will never crave the love of a man, that you will never again face the ache of loneliness? No. But Jesus wants to be your all in all—He wants to meet you in your loneliness and to be your refuge, your peace, your joy. He wants you to move deeper into intimacy with Him.

Many women through the centuries have delighted in the intimacy and ecstasy available to every believer with their eternal bridegroom. Madam Guyon, a French woman who lived in the 1600s, experienced a passionate union with Jesus and was imprisoned for her "extreme views." We like this radical lady. She understood the joy of spiritual oneness and encourages us to ask God for this understanding.

> Your spirit is perfectly made to be united with God.... You truly
> are made to be married to Him. Your spirit can be united to God
> in this way because that is what it is made for. Deep and lasting
> union with God, the spiritual marriage, is what you should ask of
> your Beloved.[1]

Are you still skeptical? Are you wondering how such ethereal concepts as these translate into the realities of everyday life? Turn to the next chapter, and read the moving story of our dear friend Patti, who came to understand the intimacy that was hers in her relationship with Jesus.

Chapter 26

Patti: One Woman's Love

Patti, a dear friend of ours, came to understand Jesus as her beloved in a very real and tangible way. As a widow with young children, Patti went through a terribly lonely time. A gaping hole filled her heart, but she learned to let Jesus fill that hole. We'll let her tell her story.

My sweet husband of ten years had been ripped from my life when the fighter jet he was piloting plunged into the Adriatic Sea. Packing up my three preschoolers and moving from Italy back to the United States, I knew I would need God in ways I never had before. I was sure God would be with us. His Word continually exposes His compassion for the widow and the fatherless. But could He really be my husband as well? How could an invisible God hold me and love me as I longed to be loved? I wasn't sure how He would do it but was determined to give Him the opportunity to show me.

I knew that if God was going to be my husband and my lover, then I definitely ought to get to know Him better. So night after night, when my little ones were safely tucked in bed, I met with Him by the fireplace and read the epistles, God's love letters to me. I kept a journal of His qualities. After writing down just a few of them, it became crystal clear to me that I was an undeserving bride of the perfect bridegroom. God's perfection stood in sharp contrast to my own imperfections: His graciousness beside my unworthy heart, His holiness alongside my soiled soul, and His matchless strength towering above my needy posture typified the unlikely union.

Humbled, I continued to read of His tender, undying love for me. I talked to Him, cried with Him, shook my fist at Him, and fell asleep next to Him every night. Emotionally and spiritually, God became my husband. He found ways to hold me and love me, as I needed so desperately.

I savored my time with Him, knowing He was preparing me for an abundant life ahead whether as a widow or as a wife. Either way, I didn't want to miss this sweet time with Him. Every moment spent with God deepened my love for Him and intensified my trust of Him. But God knew of my desire to remarry. I acknowledged this before Him and then had to constantly lay that desire back at His feet. In time, my prayer became:

God's man in God's timing for God's purposes—or no man at all.

The more familiar I became with God's face, the easier I knew it would be to recognize His face in a potential suitor. I wanted a Spirit-filled man to be the spiritual head of my home. How better to recognize if the suitor was Spirit-filled than for me to know the Holy Spirit personally?

With a ten-year marriage under my belt, I understood that even if God were to bring a new, wonderful, Spirit-filled man into my life again, my perfect lover and husband would always remain Jesus. Only embraced by Jesus' profoundly perfect, unrelenting love would I have the capacity to give an earthly husband the freedom to be human. Time has taught me that the best helpmates aren't those who play Holy Spirit with their husbands, but rather those who are filled with the Holy Spirit. Whether God wanted me to be a Spirit-filled widow or a Spirit-filled wife, I could see no downside in faithfully pursuing an intimate relationship with my first love.[1]

PATTI'S VALENTINE POEM

Patti knew the joy of spiritual oneness with her bridegroom. She also knew the loneliness single, widowed, and divorced women feel on Valentine Day. Wives and sweethearts receive flowers, candy, and cards dripping with words of love on Valentine Day, but the woman alone receives no affirmations of love, no thoughtful bouquets. Patti knew this loneliness and one Valentine Day laid her loneliness at the feet of Jesus and wrote the following poem.

To God, My Husband.[2]
How can I possibly write a love letter
To the One whose name is Love?
For I know the love I have for You
Is but a poor reflection of Your love for me.

All my words of love, straight from the heart,
Regardless of their eloquence and depth,
Dim in the shadow of Your pure, brilliant love,
A love that knows no bounds.

You have been my stronghold,
The One in whom I put my trust.
When all other relationships fade away,
You remain with me, always.

You have loved me when I'm unlovable;
You have been faithful through my unfaithfulness.
You alone have seen the depth of my ugliness,
And found beauty in me when no one else could.

You have listened to my continuous grumbling
And the accusations I've thrown at You in ignorance.

You have never forced Your love on me,
But have waited patiently for me to accept it.

There is no doubt that Your love for me
Is completely undeserved.
Rather, it is a gift You have given me, freely,
For I have no means to earn it.

Your unconditional love for me
Is what I desire above life itself.
Without it, I am but an empty vessel
Which can never be adequately filled.

But my love for You has limitless potential
As long as it reflects You, Love itself.
I LOVE You, my Bridegroom, with all my heart.

Jesus is Patti's friend, leader, and lover. When you read her story and poem, does your spirit say, "Yes, I long for this too"? Or do you pull back because too much intimacy (into-me-see) frightens you.

Many women say they want a deep relationship with Jesus, but they keep Him at arm's length, treating Him more like a date than a mate. They settle for occasional encounters with Him—going to a Christian concert or enjoying time together at a church retreat. After the "date," they tell their friends that Jesus is wonderful and that they want to spend more time with Him, but still they hesitate. Something about intimacy simultaneously attracts and repels them. One part of them is desperate for love—to know and be known by Him—the other part is desperately afraid.

Jesus wants to slip the ring on your finger and to speak of His undying love for you (Jeremiah 31:3). Will you accept the ring and promise love in return, or will you bolt like the runaway bride?

If you have the urge to run, ask yourself why. What is it about commitment that frightens you? Is it the feeling that you will fail, that you could never live up to the high standards of being the bride of Christ? Are you afraid that total commitment to Jesus would require too much sacrifice on your part? Maybe you've given yourself to someone in the past, and they rejected you, and the only way you know to protect yourself from pain is to hold back from total commitment.

Don't be afraid. God loves you with a burning love, a blazing passion. He would never do anything to harm you, because the fire of bridal love burns in Him. He wants this same fire to burn in you. Listen to this beautiful description of bridal love:

> From eternity past, there is a fiery furnace of love that has been limited to but Three. The Father, Son, and Holy Ghost have enjoyed an affection of astronomical proportions that is so fiery in its intensity and scope that no other creature would even dare step into this blazing furnace of divine love. Oh the love that draws the Father into the heart of the Son, and the Spirit into the heart of the Father, and the Son into the heart of the Spirit! And now, as the angels gaze into this blazing inferno, they see the form of a fourth walking in the midst of the fire. And this fourth person has the appearance of the bride of Christ![3]

Jesus demonstrated His great love for you by dying for you and enveloping you in the eternal blazing love of the Triune God. How can you love Him in return?

Jesus was asked, "Which is the greatest commandment? (Matthew 22:36, NIV). Did He answer: "Love the Lord with most of your heart, part of your mind, a bit of your soul, and with as much strength as you can muster after doing everything else in your life"? Of course, that is *not* how our Lord responded, but that is how many of us interpret Jesus' words!

Your bridegroom asks you to love Him totally—with all of your being. Will you accept the ring of commitment and love Him with:

All your heart?

All your mind?

All your soul?

All your strength?

Ask the Holy Spirit to breathe on the coals of your life and ignite a new flame of passion in you. Tell the Spirit that you are not satisfied, that you want more of Jesus, that you want to be consumed by Him. Be abandoned in your love for Jesus, and in that abandonment something new will stir inside you. You will feel the birth of a new passion for Jesus. You will experience the joy of Jesus as your bridegroom! We encourage you to express your love to Him by beginning and ending each day with this simple prayer:

Lord Jesus, my bridegroom, I love You.
Increase my love for You.
Show me experientially what it means
that You are my bridegroom NOW.
Lead me into deeper intimacy with You.

Chapter 27

Adorn Your Wedding Clothes

Remember young Madeline—she stood before a mirror and gazed in wonder at her make-believe wedding finery? Each part of her white ensemble—the towel veil, the chiffon gown, the oversized pumps—contributed to her feeling like a bride.

Madeline was a make-believe bride putting on garments from her dress-up box. But you are a true bride putting on heavenly garments. Hard to believe? We did not make this up. It's in God's Word. Look with us at this beautiful passage from Revelation that describes your bridal attire.

> "Let us rejoice and be glad and give the glory to Him, for the marriage of the Lamb has come and His bride has made herself ready." It was given to her to clothe herself in fine linen, bright and clean; for the fine linen is the righteous acts of the saints. (Revelation 19:7-8)

We see two important concepts in this passage. One: The bride makes *herself* ready—no one can do this for her. Two: Her linen clothes symbolize righteous acts.

Let's look first at how the bride makes herself ready. To understand this, we must go back to the idea previously discussed that God often uses a small story to portray a larger story.

THE SMALL STORY: A PURE BRIDE ON EARTH

Your story is the small story. It involves what you are doing right now to prepare yourself to become an earthly bride. As you have read this book, you have made choices. You have either said yes or no to following God and to saving the Gift. Each yes you declared before God was a righteous act. Each yes was like putting on a part of the linen wedding dress. Think back to every choice you have made as you have read this book.

When you said:

Yes! I will commit to sexual purity, you put on linen undergarments.

Yes! I will live my vision statement, you put on the linen slip.

Yes! I will set my heart on God, you put on the linen skirt.

Yes! I will renew my mind with God's Word, you put on the linen blouse.

Yes! I will control my body, you tied in place the linen belt.

Yes! I will strengthen my will, you adorned yourself with wedding jewelry.

Yes! I will resist the Enemy, you put on linen gloves.

Yes! I will accept Your timetable, you put on the wedding veil.

How do you look? As we view you in our hearts, you look beautiful, bright, clean, and pure! Each time you said yes to God, you covered yourself with God's purity. With each yes you put on holy character. As you live out the small story of making choices and putting on the linen garments, it not only prepares you for your earthly bridegroom but also for your heavenly bridegroom.

THE LARGER STORY: A PURE BRIDE IN HEAVEN

You may be tempted to view your small acts of obedience as having little significance to anyone but you, but *this is not true*. Each earthly choice you make has a heavenly connection. Lift your eyes. See the larger story. Understand that each choice you make to be a pure bride on earth is a contribution to the larger story of the spiritual bride making herself ready for her bridegroom.

Do you see? Two things happen at once. Your small story of obedience on earth becomes a higher, heavenly story. One day you will be at the marriage supper of the Lamb. On that day, that glorious joyful day, you will see how your choices contributed to the spiritual bride making herself ready.

> It will be a most impressive gathering. Nothing will be spared to celebrate the victory of those in attendance. The King Himself will take off His robes and serve them. No conclave has ever been more magnificent; more rejoicing has never been witnessed. They gather to remember and give thanks at this, the wedding feast of the Lamb.[1]

Does this excite you? We pray it stirs your heart and gives you a higher purpose for your obedience. You are not just plodding along here on earth, making hard choices, waiting…waiting… *The angels are watching. Your choice to be a pure bride has eternal significance!*

Each choice you have made to put on the linen garments delights God's heart. He is pleased with your obedience. He says:

> *"Well done."*

What could be more glorious than to have our Lord say, "Well done"? Is there anything in life that could be more rewarding, more satisfying? Oh, to please God. This is the cry of our hearts. We believe this is your desire as well. You are making choices to follow Him in the present. God urges you to continue to be faithful in the future.

FOREVER FAITHFUL

> **I have chosen** the faithful way.…
> **I cling** to Your testimonies.…
> **I shall run** the way of Your commandments,
> For You will enlarge my heart. (Psalm 119:30-32)

Psalm 119 describes David's desire to live according to God's Word. In this passage, David summarizes the scope of his intent—to follow God's ways in the past, present, and future.

In the past: "**I have chosen** the faithful way." *Chosen* in Hebrew means to "take a keen look at." It is a choosing that has ultimate and eternal significance.[2] Your choice in the past to set your heart on God's path of purity and to save the Gift has eternal significance. God rejoices over your choice.

In the present: "**I cling** to Your testimonies." *Cling* is a strong word that means to "stick like glue." It is the word translated *cleave* in Genesis 2:24 (KJV) concerning marriage: "Therefore shall a man leave his father and his mother, and shall cleave unto his wife: and they shall be one flesh." Perhaps someday you will cleave to an earthly husband, but today you "stick like clue" to your heavenly bridegroom and affirm your choice to save the Gift.

In the future: " **I shall run** the way of Your commandments." To run is to hasten toward something. Figuratively, it means to charge into battle. Your God desires that you have a "charging into battle" mentality as you live out saving the Gift, guarding the Gift, and seeking the higher Gift. With a steadfast heart, determine to keep on keeping on, running purposefully along the track of His commands.

GOD IS WORKING FOR YOU

We just saw in this psalm the importance of faithfulness in the past, present, and future. Faithfully running in the path of God's commandments —this is your part. But God has a part too!

> I shall run the way of Your commandments, for You will enlarge
> my heart. (Psalm 119:32)

As you run, God enlarges your heart by expanding your understanding.[3] He multiplies insight. He increases knowledge. When you first began reading this book, you may not have even thought about the fact that God gift-wrapped you from birth for a purpose, a purpose tied to a larger, heavenly gift. But with each page you have read, God has enlarged your heart, adding understanding, insight, and knowledge.

But God knows that this race can be long and grueling. On days when choosing His path seems impossible, God holds you up. On days when you have no strength to choose, God carries you in His strong arms. His mighty Holy Spirit who indwells you continually empowers, encourages, and motivates you. He enlarges your heart by giving you increased understanding and desire.

SARAH'S JOURNAL

Sarah is twenty-one and single. After she read the manuscript of this book, God enlarged her heart and increased her understanding and desire to save the Gift. Even though she was not dating anyone seriously, she felt impressed by God to write a letter to her future husband.

To my beloved,

I love you and only you. I can't wait to be in your arms and to be able to feel your love. You are everything I ever wanted and so much more. God knew that we would be together before we were ever born. Isn't it amazing to know that we were destined to be together before we were even alive? God is so incredible, and I thank Him so much for our love.

Isn't it so neat to think about the things that God puts in our hearts and minds? For example, you have an image of true beauty, and that is me (at least I am really hoping that), and I have an image of true beauty in a man, who is you. I think that you are the most handsome, appealing, and perfect man. You are the one who makes my heart jump and butterflies flutter in my stomach. Your warm touch causes my whole body to come alive for you. You are my beloved, and I wait for the day when we will forever be together. No combination of words can express how much I truly love you.

As we read Sarah's words, we looked at each other and realized we both had the same thought: These words could have been written by us to our eternal bridegroom, Jesus.

He is our Beloved.

He is our first love.

He is everything we have ever wanted, the perfect Man.

His touch causes us to long for deeper intimacy.

We desire to be forever in His presence, where there are pleasures evermore.

Do you see? Do you catch the unspeakable joy, the pleasures that are yours in Christ?

Deep intimacy is available to you NOW in Jesus!

As you've been reading this book, we have been praying for you. We have been asking God to give you His perspective about the Gift and to help you understand the beauty and joy that is yours in the higher Gift. Close your eyes and listen with your heart. Can you see our hands extended over you in blessing? Listen carefully with your spirit. Can you hear the words we whisper before the throne of God?

Most Holy God, we bring to You this precious one.
We ask You to encourage her
as she daily chooses to save the Gift.
May she fully enter into the joy of knowing Jesus
as her bridegroom. May He truly be her ALL in ALL!

The Spirit and the bride say, "Come."
And we say, "Yes, Lord Jesus, come!"
(Revelation 22:17)

Eight~Week Bible Study

Dear Friend,

Many young women read a book such as this one and excitedly think, *Yes, I want God's perspective about sex—I want to honor God with my actions.* But as the days pass, their enthusiasm and commitment wane because they fail to immerse themselves in the Scriptures and to allow the Spirit of God to perform lasting change in their lives. We applaud you for taking that extra step—for opening yourself up to a deeper work of God by committing to do this Bible study. We pray that in the weeks to come you will look back and say, "I'm so glad I did this study. God has changed me!"

Purpose

The purpose of this eight-week study is to saturate your heart and mind with God's Word so that your sexual attitudes may be conformed to God's attitude. You will need a copy of this book, a Bible, and a notebook in which to record your answers. You can do the study on your own or in a group, but we recommend a group setting because we feel you would greatly benefit from interaction with other single women. Those who desire additional study will enjoy the Delve Deeper section at the end of each lesson.

Guidelines

If you are joining with others for this study, we encourage you to ask each woman to commit to the following guidelines during your initial meeting.

1. *Keep the study centered on God.* Begin and end your time in worship and prayer. Share what you are learning about God and His perspective on sex or on what God is personally teaching you.

2. *Agree to confidentiality.* Make certain each woman agrees that what is shared in the group *stays* in the group and that no information will be shared without express permission.

3. *Use wisdom in sharing.* Because of the sensitive nature of this study, it is important that you use discretion in sharing. Ask God to show you what is permissible to share and what is not. He will be your guide.

When we went through this study with a group of single women, we repeatedly heard comments such as:

"I have a whole new perspective on sex and waiting for marriage."

"God has given me a new beginning sexually."

"Finally, I have the tools to help me wait for marriage."

We pray your group will enjoy similar revelations. May God richly bless your time in His Word as you seek to know His perspective.

Linda &
Lorraine

Lesson One

So let us celebrate the festival...by eating the new bread of purity and truth.
1 CORINTHIANS 5:8, NLT

Read Section One (Chapters 1-5)
1. Memorize Ephesians 5:31-32. Write these verses in your notebook.
2. Write one paragraph describing the world's view of sex and one paragraph describing God's view.
3. Reread the six reasons God gave the Gift of sex to married couples (pages 18-22). Write at least two new insights you gleaned.
4. Throughout Scripture, God uses physical pictures to portray spiritual truths. Look up the following Scripture references and fill in the chart. The first example is done for you.

VERSES	PHYSICAL PICTURE	SPIRITUAL PICTURE
John 10:7-9	Gate/Door	Jesus is gate (opening) for eternal life
John 15:5		
Matthew 26:26-29		
Genesis 22:8; John 1:29		
Ephesians 5:31-32		

5. Write a paragraph describing why you think God chose the sexual relationship in marriage to portray spiritual intimacy.
6. Describe the most special gift you've ever been given. What made the gift so meaningful?
7. How does the possibility of giving your body as a Gift on your wedding night make you feel? Write five adjectives.

Delve Deeper
8. What did you learn about God this week? about yourself? Write a prayer to the Lord describing what you learned.

Lesson Two

Therefore there is now no condemnation for those who are in Christ Jesus.
For the law of the Spirit of life in Christ Jesus has set you free
from the law of sin and of death.

ROMANS 8:1-2

Read Section Two (Chapters 6-11)

1. Memorize 2 Corinthians 5:17. Write this verse here, inserting your name in place of the words *anyone* and *he*. What emotions fill your heart when you see your name written in this verse? List two.

2. Read John 3:16 and 1 Corinthians 6:19.
   a. What did it cost Christ to purchase your redemption?
   b. Have you personally received Jesus Christ as your Savior from sin? If so, write a short description of how you received Christ.

3. According to 1 Corinthians 6:13, what is your body meant for? What is it NOT meant for?

4. Read 1 Corinthians 6:18 and the section on soul ties (pages 41-44). List two ways sexual sin is different from other sin.

5. Ask God to reveal any soul ties you have with another person. Go through the prayer on pages 52-53, and ask Him to cut each tie.

6. Read and meditate on Ephesians 5:3-5.
   a. Name the sexual sins mentioned in these verses.
   b. Practically, what does it mean to you that there should not even be a *hint* of sexual immorality or any impurity among you?

7. Describe a situation where you responded inappropriately when you were "pulled in" to an off-color joke or sexual gossip about another person.

8. Describe a situation where you responded appropriately when you were "pulled in" to an off-color joke or sexual gossip about another person.

Delve Deeper

9. Write out your personal testimony of how you received Jesus Christ as your personal Savior, using these three statements as your outline.
    • Before I became a Christian…
    • How I became a Christian…
    • After I became a Christian…

10. Many women have suffered the agony of sexual abuse. If you have not been sexually abused, spend some time praying for specific women you know who suffer this pain. If you have been sexually abused, know that God weeps with you. AND He longs to redeem your deep pain. Will you

    a. commit to read one book listed on page 64 that deals with sexual abuse? This will encourage you in your path to healing.

    b. reread Natalie's story (pages 59-65)? Write a prayer to God, thanking Him that just as He set Natalie free, His desire is to set you free. Be honest with Him about where you are, asking Him to meet you and take you toward total healing.

Lesson Three

Look straight ahead, and fix your eyes on what lies before you.
Mark out a straight path for your feet; then stick to the path and stay safe.
PROVERBS 4:25-26, NLT

Read Chapters 12-13

1. Read and meditate on Proverbs 4:25-26 (see above).

2. Set aside an hour to be quiet and alone with the Lord. Reread chapter 12, "Capturing the Vision." Ask God to give you His wisdom concerning your personal vision statement.

3. Write your own personal vision statement of who you desire to be on your wedding day. This can be in the form of a poem, an acrostic, a contract, a song, or even a simple paragraph. Be creative! See pages 75-76 for ideas.

4. Your vision statement is IMPORTANT! Rewrite your vision statement in a "keepsake" format so that you can see and review it often. It can be written on a card placed in your Bible, framed and placed on your dresser, or made into a bookmark.

5. Share your vision statement with a friend. Read it to her, then ask her to pray with you and hold you accountable to your vow. If you are meeting with a study group, come prepared to share what you have written.

Delve Deeper

6. Write a letter to a friend living in another city or state challenging her to consider writing her personal vision statement for sexual purity. Be sure to include a copy of your vision statement as a sample.

Lesson Four

Do not conform any longer to the pattern of this world,
but be transformed by the renewing of your mind.

ROMANS 12:2, NIV

Read Chapters 14-15

1. Memorize Romans 12:2. Then write your personal paraphrase of this verse.

2. What keeps you from loving God and putting Him first in your heart? Make a list of anyone or anything that competes with God for your love and devotion.

3. Reread Lorraine's pledge on pages 85-87. Then write a pledge to God of your desire to have Him first in your heart.

4. Turn to pages 90-92, and reread the section "Set Your Heart on Loving." Complete the following statements taken from 1 Corinthians 13, personalizing each with ways you can reach out to the special one in your life. (If there is no special one, think of ways you can do this for a close friend.)

   Love is patient: "I can…"

   Love is kind: "I can…"

   Love is not jealous: "I can…"

   Love is not rude: "I can…"

   Love does not demand its own way: "I can…"

   Love is not irritable: "I can…"

   Love never gives up: "I can…"

   Love is always hopeful: "I can…"

6. Reread the section "Set Your Heart on Prayer" on pages 92-94. Choose from one of the following prayer exercises (wisdom principles from Proverbs, fruit of the Spirit from Galatians, or love principles from 1 Corinthians), and practice applying it this week

either with your boyfriend/fiancé or a close friend. Write a short paragraph sharing what you learn as you do this.

7. Draw a picture of your sexual mind-set using the flower bed image described on pages 96-97.

    a. First draw a line that will represent the bare soil of your mind when you were born—no images relating to sexuality.

    b. How did you first hear about sex? Did it produce a weed or a flower? Draw it now.

    c. Go through all the years until the present—comments you heard, things you saw, situations you experienced—and draw a weed or flower for each. You now have a picture of your sexual mind-set. (Don't forget to include the flowers you have planted while reading this book.)

    d. Write five words that describe your sexual mind-set.

8. *Uproot the weeds.* In John 15:1, God is described as a gardener. Write a short prayer asking the Gardner to uproot the weeds in your mind. As you write, know that regardless of whether your weeds are small or large, few or plenty, God can make your mind a place of beauty, color, and fragrance.

9. *Plant flower seeds.* The barren places can now be filled in with beautiful, colorful flowers (verses) of God's Word in your mind.

    a. Choose three verses from "Flower Seeds" on pages 102-103 that you would like to memorize. Write them down.

    b. Pick one of the verses written under (a) and write a prayer praying this verse back to God.

Delve Deeper

10. What does it mean that purity should be a "lifelong attitude"?

11. Reread "Benefits of Purity" (page 89) and "Why Wait?" (pages 47-48). Make your own lists:

    a. By pursuing purity I will be free from:

    b. By pursuing purity I will be free to:

Lesson Five

> ***Flee** from anything that stimulates youthful lust.*
> ***Follow** anything that makes you want to do right.*
> *Pursue faith, love, and peace. **Find** companions*
> *who call on the Lord with pure hearts*
> 2 TIMOTHY 2:22, our paraphrase

Read Chapters 16-17

1. Memorize 2 Timothy 2:22. Write it here.
2. Complete the following fifteen-minute life-changing exercise:
   Reread the description of Lorraine's mirror exercise on pages
   108-110. Then write out Psalm 139:14, and tape it to your
   bathroom mirror. Stand in front of the mirror, take off your
   clothes, and thank God for every part of your body. Start
   with the top of your head, and go all the way down to your
   toes, praising God that you are "fearfully and wonderfully
   made."
3. Read 1 Thessalonians 4:1-4. Personalize this passage by rewriting
   it, inserting your name, and applying it to you.
4. Read the section entitled "The Path of Purity" on pages 114-119.
   Select two commitments from the following list, and write a short
   paragraph describing how you will
   • stay at the feet of Jesus
   • stay active and exercise your body
   • pour yourself into the lives of others
   • join a discipleship program or Bible study
   • be accountable to an older woman or mentor
5. Three keywords are included in your memory verse (2 Timothy
   2:22): *flee, follow,* and *find.*
   a. List three ways you can *flee* sexual passion.

    b. Write three things that will encourage you to *follow* God's plan.

    c. Consider what you can do now to *find* friends who will help you in your commitment to follow God's path of purity (Psalm 119:63).

6. Read "I Will Follow" on pages 123-128.

    a. Describe your dress boundaries.

    b. Describe your time boundaries.

    c. Describe your touch boundaries.

7. Write a prayer to God expressing your desire to "run straight to the goal with purpose in every step" (1 Corinthians 9:26, NLT). Express the changes you want to put in place that will help ensure your victory. Ask for His strength and empowerment as you run.

Delve Deeper

8. Memorize Psalm 139:14, and pray it back to God every day for a week.

9. What did you learn about God this week? What did you learn about yourself? Write a prayer to God expressing what you have learned and then call a friend and share it with her.

Lesson Six

Be of sober spirit, be on the alert. Your adversary, the devil,
prowls around like a roaring lion, seeking someone to devour.
But resist him, firm in your faith.

1 PETER 5:8-9

Read Section 4 (Chapters 18-21)

1. Memorize James 4:7: "Resist the devil and he will flee from you."
2. Read Ezekiel 28:12-17.
    a. Describe Satan's created role.
    b. Describe Satan's created character.
    c. Describe Satan's created appearance.
3. Read Genesis 3:1-8. Eve's temptation progressed through three stages (page 147 explains these stages). Describe Eve's choices and actions in each stage:
    * temptation
    * contemplation
    * activation
4. Read Genesis 3:8-24.
    a. List the consequences that occurred because of Eve's failure to say no to temptation.
    b. How did Eve's choice affect others?
    c. If you give in to sexual temptation, who would be affected by your choices and how? Make a list.
5. Three lies were discussed in chapter 19. Choose one of these (or write your own), and write a short statement of truth to counteract Satan's lie. Use scripture to substantiate the truth.
    * Satan is a harmless Halloween character.
    * God withholds good from me.
    * There is no battle over my sexual purity.

6. Reread the section "Spiritual Caller ID" on pages 154-157. Write a paragraph detailing how you can apply in your life the two questions, Is the thought true? Does the thought please God?

7. You are told to use the Word of God as your offensive weapon against your enemy. Reread the section "The Sword of God's Word" on pages 157-159. Choose two scriptures, and show how you will use them as a "sword" against Satan.

Delve Deeper

1. Read Isaiah 14:12. List five sins Satan committed against his Creator.

2. Read John 8:44; 1 Peter 5:8; Revelation 12:10; and 2 Corinthians 11:14-15.
   • Describe Satan's current role.
   • Describe Satan's fallen character.
   • Describe Satan's appearance.

3. Read Ephesians 6:13-17. Write a phrase describing each piece of the armor and its role in helping you battle your enemy.

4. One of Satan's greatest tools is discouragement. Think back to a time when you felt defeated and discouraged.
   a. How could you have defeated Satan by raising the banner of praise?
   b. Write a prayer of praise here.

Lesson Seven

Let us rejoice and be glad and give him glory!
For the wedding of the Lamb has come,
and his bride has made herself ready.
Fine linen, bright and clean, was given her to wear.
REVELATION 19:7-8, NIV

Read Sections Five and Six (Chapters 22-27)

1. Memorize Revelation 19:7-8. Note that "fine linen" stands for the righteous acts of the saint.

2. As you read chapters 22-23, what went through your mind? Can you relate to some of the ideas shared by Patti Ann, Jill, and Nancy? Write a short paragraph describing your thoughts.

3. Read Psalm 37:1-7. Complete the following statements based on these verses. As I wait:

   a. I will trust in the Lord and do good by

   _____.

   b. I will be at peace where God puts me by

   _____.

   c. I will delight in the Lord by

   _____.

   d. I will commit my life totally and unreservedly to the Lord by

   _____.

   e. I will trust in Him by

   _____.

   f. I will be quiet before the Lord by

   _____.

   g. I will wait patiently for Him by

   _____.

4. Write a short paragraph from each of the following verses expressing what each means to you personally as you wait.
   a. Psalm 31:14-15a
   b. Isaiah 64:4
   c. Isaiah 40:31

5. Second Corinthians 11:2 says that you are the bride of Christ. Describe how this makes you feel.

6. As you read the Scriptures and examples we shared concerning intimacy with Jesus, what were your reactions? Were you encouraged? Discouraged? Does the prospect of intimacy with Jesus intrigue you or frighten you? Write a paragraph expressing your thoughts.

7. Pick one of the following three aspects of knowing Jesus as your bridegroom, and write what this looks like for you personally:
   a. Jesus, your bridegroom, is your friend.
   b. Jesus, your bridegroom, is your leader.
   c. Jesus, your bridegroom, is your lover.

8. Write your memory verses (Revelation 19:7-8) here.
   a. Personalize the verse, rewriting it as a prayer to your bridegroom.
   b. Make a list of your righteous acts that have made you ready to be His bride.

9. Read Psalm 119:30-32. How do you plan to keep running the way of His commandments? List at least five ways.

Delve Deeper

10. Write a letter to your future husband expressing your desire to save the Gift for him and how you plan to do this.

Lesson Eight

Give thanks to the LORD, call upon His name;
make known His deeds among the peoples.
Sing to Him, sing praises to Him; speak of all His wonders.
Glory in His holy name;
let the heart of those who seek the LORD be glad.

PSALM 105:1-3

For seven weeks you have studied about the Gift—how to recapture the Gift, save the Gift, guard the Gift, and the importance of seeing the higher Gift. Week eight is a time to offer thanksgiving and to celebrate what God has revealed to you.

Thanksgiving

(Do this section on your own, prior to meeting with your group.)

1. Begin each day by thanking God for something He has taught you during the past seven weeks.

2. Review all you have studied during the past seven weeks. Write several paragraphs expressing what you have learned *about God.* Praise God for what He has taught you through His Word.

3. Write several paragraphs expressing what you have learned *about yourself.* Thank God for what He has revealed about your attitudes and actions.

4. Prepare something special to share with your group during your celebration time. Be creative! Allow the talents God has given you to bless others. Here are some suggestions.

   • Read something you wrote for an assignment.

   • Write a song, a poem, or a letter to God thanking Him for what He has shown you.

- Make an acrostic using a word like *gift* or *intimacy*.
- Cite from memory a passage of Scripture that has been meaningful to you.
- Paint a picture of the new flower bed in your mind.

Celebration (Group Time)

Your time of celebration will be during your final group time. Decide in advance how this time will look (consider having a meal together at someone's home). Allow time for each woman to share how this study has impacted her.

1. Begin your time with worship and prayer. Ask God to bless your celebration.
2. Have each woman share what she has prepared.
3. End with a time of worship and prayer, celebrating what God has done.

Notes

Chapter 1: Confusing Voices

1. Gregg Zoroya, "Beachhouse Escapism, East Coast-style," *USA Today;* 5 July 2001.
2. Laura Vanderkam, "Hookups Starve the Soul," *USA Today,* 26 July 2001.

Chapter 4: The Gift Exchange

1. The wedding night passage is found in Song of Solomon 4:1-5:1.
2. Joseph Dillow suggests that "garden" is probably a euphemism for the female genitals; Joseph C. Dillow, *Solomon on Sex* (Nashville: Nelson, 1977), 81.
3. Ron Allen, *Worship: The Missing Jewel of the Christian Church* (Portland: Multnomah, 1982), 120.

Chapter 5: God's Voice on Sex

1. Adapted from "What Does God Think About Sex?" in Linda Dillow and Lorraine Pintus, *Intimate Issues* (Colorado Springs: WaterBrook, 1999), 6-10.
2. See Genesis 4:1.
3. Genesis 4:1 (NKJV): "Now Adam knew [had sexual intercourse with] Eve his wife, and she conceived and bore Cain."
4. Proverbs 5:8
5. 1 Peter 1:8

Chapter 6: "For This He Died"

1. John Murray, "Redemption," in the *International Standard Bible Encyclopedia* (Grand Rapids: Eerdmans, 1988), 4:62.
2. Adapted from a true story.
3. The Greek word *tetelesti* ("it is finished") means "paid in full."

Chapter 7: Kendall: One Woman's Journal

1. "Kendall" and "Casey" are fictitious names, but the people are real. With Kendall's permission we have added certain journal entries in order to explain some of the events in her life.
2. See chaper 4.

Chapter 9: Cutting the Ties of Sexual Sin

1. *The Bible Knowledge Commentary* suggests that this woman was "probably a prostitute." Matthew Henry's Bible commentary calls her the town "harlot." The events of her encounter with Jesus are recorded in Scripture. Though we have tried to remain true to the record, the account we present here is our interpretation of the biblical event and not meant to serve as a final interpretation of what actually transpired.
2. Though Simon had neglected to show Jesus respect by washing Jesus' feet, as was the custom, God honors His Son by sending this woman to wash His feet with her tears.
3. "Sopros," in W. F. Arndt and F. W. Gingrich, *A Greek-English Lexicon of the New Testament and Other Early Christian Literature* (Chicago: University of Chicago Press, 1957), 749. The term was used of "spoiled fish."

Chapter 10: Can I Become a Virgin Again?

1. Ceslas Spico, *Theological Lexicon of the New Testament* (Peabody, Mass.: Hendrickson, 1994), 51.
2. Adapted from Tim Stafford, "Why Wait?" *Campus Life Magazine* (July-August 1987): 36-7.
3. *New Lexicon Webster's Dictionary,* s.v. "commit."

Chapter 11: Natalie: One Woman's Healing

1. Ephesians 3:17-18 (paraphrase)
2. We changed Natalie's name in order to protect her anonymity. She has given us permission to tell her story.

3. We have changed Joe's name to protect his anonymity. We have his permission to tell his story.

Chapter 12: Capturing the Vision

1. Steven Covey, *The Seven Habits of Highly Effective People* (New York: Simon & Schuster, 1989), 99.

Chapter 14: Set Your Heart

1. J. I. Packer, *Rediscovering Holiness* (Ann Arbor, Mich.: Servant, 1992), 22.
2. R. V. G. Tasker, *The Gospel According to St. Matthew,* Tyndale New Testament Commentaries (London, England: Tyndale, 1961), 62.
3. *New Lexicon Webster's Dictionary,* s.v. "purity."
4. As quoted in Tim Stafford, "Why Wait?" *Campus Life Magazine* (July-August 1987): 37.

Chapter 15: Renew Your Mind

1. Linda Dillow and Lorraine Pintus, *Intimate Issues* (Colorado Springs: WaterBrook Press, 1999), 25.
2. Rest assured, we are not embracing some sort of Eastern philosophy when we ask you to picture things in your mind! Instead, we are following the example of Christ, who spent most of His time putting concrete images in the minds of the people through the telling of stories. We ask you to picture certain images because, in doing this, you become more involved with the scriptural principles being explained.
3. Bill Hull, *Right Thinking* (Colorado Springs: NavPress, 1985), 73.
4. Adapted from a statement by author and speaker Cynthia Heald.
5. Jim Downing, *Meditation* (Colorado Springs: NavPress, 1976), 16-27.

Chapter 16: Control Your Body

1. Alanna Nash, "Marvelous Meg," *Good Housekeeping* (July 1998): 99.
2. Pamela Reeve, *Deserts of the Heart: Finding God During the Dry Times* (Sisters, Oreg.: Multnomah, 2000), 69-81.

Chapter 17: Strengthen Your Will

1. Kevin Leman, *What a Difference a Daddy Makes* (Nashville: Nelson, 2000), 6.
2. David Blankenhorn, *Fatherless American* (New York: Basic Books, 1995), 47.

Chapter 18: Monique: One Woman's Testimony

1. 2 Corinthians 2:11

Chapter 19: Satan's Lies

1. C. S. Lewis, *The Screwtape Letters* (New York: MacMillan, 1959), 3.
2. George Barna, *Boiling Point* (Ventura, Calif.: Regal, 2001), 193.
3. William F. Arndt and F. Wilbur Gingrich, *A Greek-English Lexicon of the New Testament and Other Early Christian Literature* (Chicago: University of Chicago Press, 1952), 152.
4. *New Lexicon Webster's Dictionary*, s.v. "adversary."
5. Arndt and Gingrich, *Greek-English Lexicon*, 182.
6. *Lexicon Webster's Dictionary*, s.v. "slander."

Chapter 20: The Lure of the Tempter

1. According to Jesus, if we think of another person with lustful thoughts, we commit adultery (Matthew 5:28).

Chapter 21: Battling Your Enemy

1. Michael P. Green, *Illustrations for Biblical Preaching* (Grand Rapids: Baker, 1982), 110.
2. Hebrews 4:15 says that Jesus was tempted in *every* way, but He did not sin. We can rejoice that we have a Savior who not only understands our own temptations but will help us overcome them.
3. Dorothy Kelley Patterson, ed., *New Woman's Study Bible, New King James Version* (Nashville, Tenn.: Nelson, 1995), 27, commentary on Exodus 17:15.

Chapter 22: The Long, Lonely Wait

1. Based on Elisabeth Elliot, *Loneliness* (Nashville: Nelson, 1988), 133.
2. Elliot, *Loneliness*, 140.

Chapter 23: Nancy: One Woman's Insight

1. Mike Mason, *The Gospel According to Job* (Wheaton, Ill.: Crossway, 1994), 306.

Chapter 24: A Life-Changing Secret

1. This wonderful Hebrew word means "pause and think on that."
2. This was why Joseph's thoughts about "putting away" Mary were so painful (Matthew 1:18-19). A. R. Fausset, *Bible Cyclopaedia* (Hartford, Conn.: S. S. Scranton, 1910), 453.

Chapter 25: Jesus, Your Bridegroom

1. Jeanne Guyon, *The Song of the Bride* (Sargent, Ga.: Seed Sowers Christian Books Publishing House, n.d.), introduction.

Chapter 26: Patti: One Woman's Love

1. Six years after becoming a widow, God brought a godly widower with two children into Patti's life. Today they are married and live with their five children in Virginia. Patti would tell you that although she deeply loves her new husband, Jesus is still her first love.
2. Written on Valentine Day 1996 by Patti McCarthy.
3. Bob Sorge, *Secrets of the Secret Place* (Lee's Summit, Mo.: Oasis House, 2001), 216.

Chapter 27: Adorn Your Wedding Clothes

1. Joseph C. Dillow, *The Reign of the Servant Kings* (Hayesville, N.C.: Schoettle Publishing, 1992), 585.
2. R. Laid Harris, Gleason L. Archer Jr., Bruce Waltke, *Theological Wordbook of the Old Testament* (Chicago: Moody Press, 1980), s.v. "bahar."
3. The *New Revised Standard Version* translates verse 32 as "enlarge my understanding."

"Why settle for a little heat when you can have a raging fire? *Intimacy Ignited* shows married couples how to embrace God's fun, beautiful and holy plan for sex, as described in the Song of Solomon. An essential book. The Dillows and Pintuses deliver!"

—DENNIS RAINEY, president, Family Life

You've read a book for women, by women. Now read one by couples, for couples.

Sex plays a vital role in every healthy marriage. Yet there's more to marriage than physical attraction. If your marriage doesn't have the passion it once did, learn why romance and intimacy is all about being a servant lover.

Intimacy Ignited

by Dr. Joseph & Linda Dillow
and Dr. Peter & Lorraine Pintus

1-57683-640-1

To get your copies, visit your local bookstore,
call 1-800-366-7788, or log on to www.navpress.com.
Ask for a FREE catalog of NavPress products. Offer BPA.

NAVPRESS
BRINGING TRUTH TO LIFE
www.navpress.com